*For Ian,
in appreciation for
God's*

ACTS OF

CREATION

in him

AMERICA'S FINEST HAND CRAFTSMEN AT WORK

*With love & respect,
from
his Step-Dad*

*Please read
the "About the Other Craftsman's background"
near the back.*

Acts of Creation: America's Finest Hand Craftsmen at Work
Walt Harrington

Cover Designed by: Siori Kitajima, Sf AppWorks LLC
http://www.sfappworks.com
Formatting by Siori Kitajima and Ovidiu Vlad
for SF AppWorks LLC
E-Book Formatted by Ovidiu Vlad
Cataloging-in-Publication data for this book is
available from the Library of Congress.

ISBN-13: 978-0-9895241-6-2   ISBN-10: 0989524167
E-book published by The Sager Group LLC
info@TheSagerGroup.net   info@MikeSager.com

ACTS OF CREATION

AMERICA'S FINEST HAND CRAFTSMEN AT WORK

WALT HARRINGTON

Artifex Te Adiuva

WALT HARRINGTON'S
OTHER BOOKS

These stories first appeared in *This Old House Magazine* as part of its *"An American Craftsman"* series. They are published here with generous permission.

Dedicated to Randy Martin, Roger
Francis and Glenn Lilly, craftsmen all

CONTENTS

He is among the most famous hand craftsmen in America—
the winner of a MacArthur "genius" award whose furniture
has resided in the White House, the Smithsonian Institution's Renwick Gallery, and the homes of former presidents Jimmy Carter and Ronald Reagan. Yet Sam says he
can teach almost anyone to be an excellent furniture maker.
What he cannot teach them is how to be a good, decent
and humane enough person to raise the excellent to the
sublime. He says, "You do it because of the love."

Bob has never met a lock he couldn't pick. He is that
good. Locks speak to him, and he believes they speak to
us, telling the tale of hundreds of years of cultural transformation, from the unadorned locks of the Dark Ages,
to the elaborately etched locks of the Renaissance, to the
tumbler locks that made modern security possible. In his
Ohio basement are 7,000 locks—perhaps the largest collection in the world. With his eye-piece otoscope, steady
hands, lifetime of knowledge and mysterious intuition,
Bob knows each as a mechanism and a story.

As a devotee of poet T. S. Eliot, philosopher Soren Kierkegaard and novelist Gabriel Garcia Marquez, Chuck
is the last man you'd expect to find sawing, laying, hammering and sanding hardwood floors. Yet, when he installed his first floor years ago, "It was like changing
water to wine." The Greek philosophers mused on the
gap between the ideal and the real. In his work creating elaborate, one-of-a-kind inlaid floors, Chuck ponders
that gap every day, pursuing perfection while knowing
its achievement is impossible. But reaching for it... *oh,
what a rush.*

He is one of the world's preeminent millwrights—one of the few men who still has the knowledge and skill to repair the gargantuan oak wheels, shafts, cogs, cants, gudgeons and gears that compose the antique watermills and windmills of America and Europe. Derek is awed by his own achievements, mesmerized by the seamless way that the mastery of craft and creative intellect merge in creating objects of utility and beauty. Only one other experience evokes that sensation in him: Listening to Mozart's Clarinet Concerto K. 622.

His father—a mathematician and amateur woodworker—built 8-year-old Robert a step-stool so he could run the table saw in the home workshop where they built cabinets, chairs and chests. Young Robert once asked his father if he should repair a hidden carpentry mistake that no one would ever see. "You know it's there," his father answered, and Robert made the repair. Forty years later, he constructs the 2×4 frames of houses with the same care and precision he and his father put into building furniture. "There is nothing nicer-looking than a stick-built roof just sitting up there against the sky," he says. "It's a work of art."

He was a party-loving college dropout, slapping shingles on roofs for the money when he met a Czechoslovakian sculptor on a job at a Long Island mansion. He told Larry that labor became art when the laborer made an emotional connection to his work. Another wise man on that job told Larry that work wasn't only a way to make a living but a path to life's meaning. The chance encounters transformed the way he thought about his work, which transformed the way he *did* his work. Today, Larry's stunning copper finials, domes and weather vanes adorn some of America's most beautiful roofs—archeological evidence, he believes, of his humanity.

85 PETER GOOD: HE BUILDS BEAUTIFUL DOORS

He only builds doors. A door with wooden panels that rise to hide its windows for a couple who travels a lot. A door that blends in with a home's exterior wall so it cannot be seen by casual passersby. A door built from the railroad trestle beams on which a man played as a boy. Doors of Douglas fir, East Indian rosewood, Central African bubinga. Honduran mahogany doors built, shipped to Brazil and elaborately carved by the esteemed sculptor Paulino Lazur. "I'll create something that has never existed," Peter says of his doors. "And I'll do it all myself. I like that."

93 TEDD BENSON: THE CRAFT OF CRAFTSMANSHIP

He wrote the book on how to construct timber-frame homes—literally. Published in 1980, *Building the Timber Frame House* made Tedd the cult icon of a burgeoning movement to create homes with the plain majesty of Scandinavian stave churches and Colonial meeting houses. The elaborate beam joinery of the structures resembles furniture-making done by a race of giants. "You are humbled by your own creation, this building that will stand for 500 years," he says. "And that feeling is what keeps me and all craftsmen doing it every day."

101 MANUEL PALOS: THE DRAGON IN THE STONE

If, in a thousand years, San Francisco lies in ruins, Manuel imagines that perhaps the giant 12-by-13-foot dragon fireplace he carved and chiseled from four tons of Mexican limestone for the home of actor Nicolas Cage may still stand. What will the people or beings examining our lost culture make of its fangs, flared nostrils and evil eyes? A giant talisman? A rendering of God? Or the devil? And what of Manuel's other monumental carvings of giant eagles, Zeus and Medusa? All he knows is this: "Anything well done lasts forever."

He must dedicate his friend Katie's small backyard clay kiln tonight. What should he say? That his own love and fascination with creating huge ceramic architectural adornments—Spanish, Pueblo and Gothic arches, ocean-wave wainscoting, Mayan baseboards, Aztec birds, flamingos, great blue herons, dolphins, Egyptian hieroglyphics, even human faces—has left him with debt and an old van? "If I were to win the lottery tomorrow, I'd do exactly what I do today," he finally says. "What I do is who I am. It's not a job. It's who I am."

We live in an era when men and women work to live—for time with their children, time for golf or fantasy football, time for reading a book or watching TV. Yet there are still those of us who live to work, who discover in work their love and gift and passion for excellence. For that, they often sacrifice many good things. But the *feeling* they get... it is a wonder to behold.

ACKNOWLEDGMENTS

ABOUT THE AUTHOR

PROLOGUE

THE CRAFTSMAN'S WAY

I'm the last guy you'd expect to find traveling the country trying to figure out the rites and ways of America's finest craftsmen. I got a battery-powered screwdriver for Christmas years ago, and it's still in the wrapper. My tool bag hasn't had a new tool in a decade. Almost 30 years ago, I gutted and renovated the second floor of my first fixer-upper. After 35 straight back-breaking 16-hour days, I calculated that I had saved $5,000—not nearly enough gain for the pain. I'm no nerd. I worked with my dad building fences and sheds as a kid. In college, I roofed houses for money. Just out of college, I patched drywall and refinished oak floors and kitchen cabinets to make my dumpy apartments pretend to elegance. I can swing a hammer okay.

But I confess: I never enjoyed it.

My wife once asked how I could have the patience to sit all day fiddling with the same five pages of writing but get frustrated enough after two minutes of hapless screw driving to toss the tool across the yard. "I don't like screw driving," I told her.

Yet men whose character and intelligence I respect have always loved to drive screws—and pound nails, cut boards, just plain build things. My best friend from high school quit his junior high teaching job a few years out of college to build decks, garages and houses for a living. My best friend from college did everything but his PhD dissertation, decided academia was hooey, and became a carpenter. He still reads tomes for fun, Kant's *Critique of Pure Reason* or Goethe's *Faust*. Then he drives off in his pick-up, straps on his work belt and frames up another house. These men always baffled me: *They love this work!*

Not me. On visits, I was the guy who handed out the tools, held the lamp in the dark crawl space, ran to the hardware store to pick up a new bottle of Elmer's glue. In my own work, I was doing the socially certified, high-status job of the journalist and university professor—dinners at the White House, interviews with the rich and famous, awards and books to my name. Yet again and again, these men and other craftsmen I knew humbled me.

I once visited my old friend from high school, and, with wonder in his voice, he told me he enjoyed nothing more than building a beautiful deck on a beautiful day. When I once visited my friend from college, I discovered he had totally renovated his rental apartment at his own expense. He said he had no choice—the space simply demanded a new configuration of rooms. Meanwhile, back at my fixer-upper, I had wisely hired a man to do my first-floor renovation. He was a country boy, my age, who'd been hammering on houses since he was a teenager. He cursed every fifth word and never went anywhere without his dog, Buddy. Then one day, he sheepishly mentioned that he didn't like my architect's plan.

He stood outside the front door facing my house and said that even before a person walked in, he should gaze all the way through the house and see the river on the back side. He walked in and began waving his arms at imaginary windows and French doors that should make the water, the woods and the house's interior blur to create the sensation of being outside even when you were inside. We nixed the architect. The house was beautiful.

Something is out of whack. We who believe that we *think* for a living break the world into thinkers and laborers. We give ourselves top billing. Yet these men I admired just didn't fit that hierarchy. They were smart. They didn't work with their hands because they had no choice; they worked with their hands because they loved it. For some reason, I needed to understand these men and men like them. I suppose we all do.

After all, they're the part of ourselves we left behind in our rush to become modern. After two years and thousands of miles traveled for *An American Craftsman*, after visiting an architectural ceramicist in Florida; a furniture-maker in Maryland; a mill-wright in Virginia; a coppersmith in Vermont; a timber-framer in New Hampshire; a fireplace mason in Maine; a locksmith and a house-framer in Ohio; a wood-floor man in Indiana; a blacksmith in Illinois; a chair-maker, an ornamental plasterer, a stone-carver and a door-maker in California, I know these people better. What makes them fine craftsmen?

Call it The Craftsman's Way.

They don't work for the money. A few of the 14 fine craftsmen I visited have become affluent from their crafts. But more common is furniture-maker Michael Seward, who earned $30,000 the year before I met him. Or Chuck Crispin, an award-winning maker of elaborately in-laid wood floors, and architectural ceramicist Peter King, who made even less. Often these incomes are earned in 60, 70, 80 hours of work a week. Yet all of them said that if they had launched their careers worrying about making a good living, they never would have invested the time it takes to get good enough to make a good living.

It's the catch-22 of craftsmanship.

If not for money, then what? That's the heart of it. Again and again, these craftsmen spoke of a *feeling* they get when they are working at their best. Like great athletes whose minds and bodies work in sync, fine craftsmen go into a "zone." Hours seem to pass in minutes. They describe the sensation as "addictive," "like a drug," "like a runner's high," "an emotional high," "hypnotic," "a waking dream," "meditative." It's this emotional payoff that makes the tiring, dirty, tedious labor of craft a joy.

As master furniture maker Sam Maloof said, "You do it because of the love."

Tools don't make the craftsman. Blacksmiths tell this derogatory joke about any blacksmith more obsessed with tools than craft: "He spends too much time polishing his anvil." Sam

Maloof once knew a man who spent decades outfitting the perfect woodworking shop. But he never built anything. Michael Seward built his first beautiful pieces of furniture with a wobbly old table saw. Peter King makes his giant slabs of clay on an ancient hand-roller. Clearly, this argument can go too far—a man can't build a house without hammer and nails. But to fine craftsmen, tools don't make a craftsman. Creativity, they believe, is the only irreplaceable tool.

Skills don't make the craftsman, either. This is awfully hard to explain. Craftsmen repeatedly told me that mastering their crafts' mechanical skills wasn't what made them fine craftsmen. That, of course, flies in the face of everything we think about craftsmanship—that it is a set of skills acquired over many years of patient, repetitive labor. "I can teach anyone to be a good woodworker," said Sam Maloof. But, he added, he can't teach anyone to have the human decency he believes it takes to be a truly fine woodworker.

Take that as symbolism. Because fine craftsmen come to master the mechanics of their crafts in the way that we come to master walking. A man supposedly once asked jazz saxophonist Charlie Parker how to become a great musician. The story goes that Parker told him to practice the scales all day, every day, for a decade and then to forget them. In other words, mechanical skills must become so second nature that they are unconscious, like walking. In other words, *anyone* can spend a decade learning the mechanics of a craft. But in the end, he will be judged only on the music he makes from the scales he has learned.

The work is always larger than life. Not one of these craftsmen believes he is working only to build a house, to renovate a watermill, to cast a plaster medallion. Each imbues his work with grander purpose—house framer Robert Reade is instilling a new generation of house-builders with the value of excellence; millwright Derek Ogden is preserving a nearly extinct body of knowledge; ornamental plasterer Lorna Kollmeyer is resurrecting and cataloguing a niche in the history of San Francisco's 19th-century Victorian age.

On and on it goes—Michael Seward wants the people who buy his furniture to experience an emotional connection to him through his furniture; Chuck Crispin wants his clients' lives to be evoked in his floor designs; timber-framer Tedd Benson wants his workers to share his exhilaration in the work; locksmith Bob Dix believes the history of mankind is played out in the history of locks; Jeff Gammelin wants people to sit before his monumental fireplaces and experience a primal memory of home and hearth; blacksmith Charles Keller wants the highly educated world to appreciate the complicated genius of not only fine blacksmiths but all fine craftsmen.

These craftsmen aren't just writing themselves large. In her book, *Uncommon Genius*, Denise Shekerjian interviews winners of the MacArthur prize, the so-called "genius award"—scientists, novelists, photographers, artists, philosophers, physicians and, the only craftsman in the crowd, Sam Maloof. She finds this quality in them all: They invest their work with a vision. Even Maloof tells her that his goal is to pass on the secrets of furniture-making to the next generation. How does "vision" create genius? "Give a man a purpose," Shekerjian writes, "and he will go forward, again and again, heartily, steadily, and creatively. . . . dreams unleash the imagination." So it is for craftsmen. Coppersmith Larry Stearns was a "party-loving roofer," as he put it. Then he met a sculptor who believed craft is raised to art when the craftsman makes an emotional connection to his work. He met a house builder who saw everything he made as archeological evidence of his own humanity. Only when these ideas—these values—began to animate Stearns' labor did he become excited enough about his work to do his best.

For years, Chuck Crispin had been laying wood floors when he signed on to do a job for one of the most exacting floor men in the country. The old guy demanded that Crispin cut his floor boards so tight they had to be pounded into place.

He had never known such exactitude. Suddenly, he was no longer laying a floor. He was testing the boundaries of perfection. Overnight, the inspiration of the old man's grand, unyielding vision of excellence transformed Crispin from mechanic to craftsman to artist.

Intelligence matters. The image of the steady, hard-working but-not-too-bright craftsman was probably always a myth—bad press from thinkers denigrating doers whose hands get dirty. But it's absolutely a myth for these craftsmen: Ten of the 14 graduated from college; only two never attended college at all. And none of them were art majors. They studied architecture and philosophy, engineering and anthropology, economics and English literature. Plasterer Lorna Kollmeyer was Phi Beta Kappa. Why should we be surprised? If craftsmen do their best work when imbued with a higher vision, then being quick with concepts, fast with ideas—being smart—has always mattered.

They can't rest on their laurels. Fine craftsmen are compelled to do their work differently each time they do it. This isn't only a commitment to constant self-improvement; it's more like a psychological obsession. They can't stop themselves. Days after Peter King has installed a one-of-kind ceramic fireplace, he starts worrying about how he'd do it differently next time—not better, differently. Jeff Gammelin tries never to build a fireplace like any he has built before. A man once asked Sam Maloof how he could make the same chair over and over. Knowing that no two of his chairs is ever exactly alike, Maloof answered, "I haven't got it right yet."

Perfection is not the goal. That's a shocker. But not one of these fine craftsmen's goals is to achieve perfection. The thrill is in approaching perfection—envisioning it, aiming for it, and then mastering the possibilities and limits of tools and materials, whether copper, iron, wood, clay, stone or plaster. Fine craftsmen are always trying to split the difference between where they are in their work and the ideal of perfection off in the distance. The goal is to get closer and closer, knowing they can't ever arrive. It is the narrowing of the gap by even razor-thin widths each time that inspires them.

The love of raw materials is forever fresh. After 25 years, Peter King still marvels at the sensuous feel of cool, wet clay in his hands. Manuel Palos, after 30 years of stone carving, still feels awe when he rubs a piece of raw marble to brilliance. Robert Reade hates to see the houses he frames covered with siding—those 2 × 4 skeletons are just so beautiful against the clouds. Who knows why, but fine craftsmen are always re-remembering the beauty of their raw materials. It's like seeing the man or woman you love forever young.

They work for themselves. Fine craftsmen are among the last of us who work for nobody. They should be as mythic as the American cowboy. They hate bureaucracy, bosses and paperwork. They mostly work alone. They punch their own clocks. If modern man is alienated from his work, craftsmen are not modern. They set their own standards and judge their work harsher than any employer. They don't crave vacations or leisure time, don't fret about being a workaholic. Work is their life, their love.

Finally, they are decent people. Over the years, I've written about politicians, actors, poets, athletes, teachers, cops, lawyers, bureaucrats—famous and infamous, rich and poor. The craftsmen I visited for *An American Craftsman* were as decent a gang as I've ever met. They were proud and humble at once. Nobody was a braggart. They laughed easily. Nobody was a back-slapper. After they talked, they listened. I've come to believe that Sam Maloof is right—you can't be a good craftsman if you aren't a good person. These people are proof.

From me to them—thinker to thinkers—I honor them. Their rites and ways are not only lessons for craft, but for life.

ONE

MICHAEL SEWARD

CHERISHING NATURE'S MISTAKES

When Michael Seward finished his first piece of furniture, a small Shaker-style glove table with delicately tapered legs, he set it in the center of his basement. A bare over-head bulb caught the roping grain of the curly maple, creating the impression of a mountainous terrain mapped in shades of dark and light. Burls seemed to float in three dimensions, and, as Michael circled the table, the wood grain appeared to move, to roll and heave like ocean waves. He studied the table for hours that day. His obsession with its beauty confounded him. He had the unnerving feeling that the table had been created from a place within him that he did not yet recognize or understand.

"I was mesmerized," he says.

Michael had first seen the curly maple boards at a lumber yard and couldn't pass them up – they were just so beautiful! – although he had no idea what he might do with them. And yet, a few months earlier, when he and his wife, Karen Holway, were skiing in Vermont, he had wandered into a bookstore and come across a collection of shop drawings by famous furniture maker Thomas Moser. Michael had thought to himself: *I understand this. I see how furniture is put together. Let me get a table saw and get to work.*

That was seven years ago. Today, he makes his living creating furniture, and he cannot imagine doing anything else. His work can be found in homes in and around Baltimore and Washington, D.C., and is displayed at the Main St. Gallery in Annapolis, Maryland.

A Michael Seward library cabinet – 60 inches high, 20 1/4 inches wide, 16 inches deep – will soon stand in my living room in a small, idiosyncratic nook next to the fireplace. It will be made from unusually wide, deeply whorled cherry boards taken from a single tree in Lancaster County, Pennsylvania. The tree, which stood next to a creek that still spawns native trout, was perhaps 75 years old in its last days. Michael can tell its story by examining the wood: Tiny insect boreholes record the tree's decline, rings are wide or narrow depending on the year's rain or drought, a deer hunter's rifle slug missed its mark and lodged in the trunk, a dark spot of bark was entombed like a body at Pompeii after a branch broke off and the wound was engulfed by fresh growth. The cabinet Michael will build from the boards is simple: a traditional design in natural cherry to match a Stickley natural cherry couch and chair already in my home.

The cost: $1,865.

"It's simple in design," Michael says. "Not so simple in execution."

It is more than a decade since Michael, now 41, decided to abandon his job as a social worker, buy a house in Baltimore, renovate it and sell it for a profit. He'd never done handy work, so he began watching Norm Abram on *This Old House*, then went to the library for books on how to drywall, miter trim, build decks and install kitchen cabinets. It took him several years to finish the house. At that point, he decided to try making the Shaker-style glove table. As he studied it in his basement, he had—how else to say it?—that epiphanic flash. With his humble eight-inch Black & Decker table saw and Elu router, he went on to build a chest of drawers, two corner tables and a jewelry chest.

"I wanted to create," he says. "I've always felt that feeling."

He sold the pieces of furniture. Then someone saw the kitchen cabinets he'd made for his house and hired him to build a kitchen. With the security of a commission in hand, his wife, who was working at a high-paying banker's job, jumped at the chance to take a buyout. They moved to the country near New Park, Pennsylvania, and, job by job, began buying tools. A planer and a jointer, chisels and knives, $75,000 in equipment so far. Last year, they sold $60,000 worth of furniture and custom kitchen cabinets and made $30,000 for themselves.

"It hasn't been easy," Karen says.

Their 1,600-square-foot shop smells of linseed oil, sawdust, machinery and, most of all, wood: cherry, birch, walnut, sugar maple and bird's-eye maple, a wood that fascinates Michael. Standing with one foot on a pile of neatly stacked rough-cut lumber, he leans down to rub mineral spirits onto a board of bird's-eye maple to reveal its swirling grain. "This is a freak of nature," he says. "Nobody knows what causes it. You have to find it by sheer chance."

A sideboard built from the same cherry log he is using for my library cabinet sits nearby, almost finished. The faces of the three cabinet drawers form a long, undulating landscape. "It gives a canvas for showing off the wood," Michael says. As he talks, he splays long, dexterous fingers and gestures with his hands in gentle, expressive arcs at his chest. The hands are worn, protected by four calluses on the palms acquired from grasping and turning clamps and tools. "Even if people don't consciously notice that the grain matches, they will notice it subconsciously. Woodworking is an ancient art, so there's nothing new in putting the furniture together. The wood is what makes it special."

Michael and Karen work together now. At first, she handled only business matters, but over the years she came to spend more and more time in the shop, measuring and cutting and sanding. Recently she too began signing each piece of furniture. As he is captivated by the visual beauty of the wood, she is enthralled by its sensual qualities, loves knowing the scent of, say, red oak versus white oak. She rubs the wood when it's rough with splinters and then rubs it again after it has been planed, when she can still feel the tiny blade cuts and nicks, and then rubs it again after she has sanded and oiled and buffed and shellacked it, then oiled and buffed it at least six more times, until it is nearly frictionless to the touch.

"There's a joy in doing it by hand," she says.

"To put yourself into the work," he says.

The pieces for my library cabinet have been cut to length and width and jointed and planed to parallel thicknesses. The cherry is dense heartwood, 16 inches wide, rare today. Also rare is the winding, salmon-colored grain that reflects light differentially, creating an illusion of depth. On the cabinet's inside back piece, Michael has showcased the dark spot where the tree's bark was enveloped by growth decades ago. Many would see this as a defect. He sees it as nature's fingerprint.

This is a simple cabinet: When all the wood is finally ripped and crosscut and the dado, rabbet, mortise, tenon and dovetail joints are cut and glued; when the brass hinges are mortised and installed and the horizontal rails and vertical stiles of the doors are cut from a single board and the inside stiles are book-matched and the door glass is installed with tiny brass pins; when the shelves are cut from one board with grain that flows like a waterfall from shelf to shelf; when the entire cabinet is sanded, oiled and buffed and the door pulls are in place and it's delivered and standing in the nook next to my fireplace, Michael and Karen will have worked 100 hours and spent $645 on materials. Their real wages: $12.20 an hour.

"We're trying to do pieces valuable enough to justify spending the time doing them for the pure joy of it," Michael says. "I'd love to be able to afford my own furniture. But that's part of the poverty of woodworking. You build these beautiful pieces, and they're gone, in somebody else's possession. The work is not inherently satisfying in and of itself. It's very tedious – a lot of noise and sawdust and aggravation. But there's something beyond that. There's something about the end of the day, when you're done.

"You've added value to the world."

That's what kept Michael going when he overheard a man at the Main St. Gallery gripe that his prices were outrageous. It's what calmed him when he cut a tenon too short or built a cabinet too boxy. It's what made him work 11-hour days, seven days a week.

Michael has always been a patient man. That is an unyielding demand of craft. But he is now more patient than ever. And he has become a better builder. He can cut a dovetail joint with little concentration now, and that has mattered not because it has made his work easier but because it has freed his mind to ponder and design, moved him closer to the source of why he felt so compelled to build furniture in the first place.

His tools are better now, and that too has mattered. So many men believe that if they only had the tools, the horsepower, they could build an elegant sideboard or library cabinet of wonder. But the tools aren't the source either. Michael built his first pieces with a table saw that wobbled so badly its 1/8-inch blade made a 1/4-inch cut. No, the source of his ability was his belief – his blind certainty – that the pure joy of adding value to the world would someday be worth the agony of apprenticeship. How did he know that?

"I have no idea," he says.

Michael has clients who earn large incomes at jobs they dislike. These unhappy people often seem to romanticize his life, imagine he works whenever he pleases. He laughs at that. He hasn't had a day off in years. "I think that one of the reasons they buy the furniture is to associate themselves with the lifestyle it represents to them." Still, most of Michael's clients aren't wealthy. They return to the gallery repeatedly to see a piece, touch it, contemplate it before they buy. As Michael was mesmerized by his first table, they too are mesmerized. They save their money, fearing that someone else might buy the piece they want. Some of them say the furniture seems to speak to them, and Michael understands. He believes that he speaks to the new owners through the furniture, touches them in some unspoken way.

He got a letter recently from a woman who bought one of his pieces. She wrote: "The table was purchased to honor the love I feel for my husband. It brings us both great joy." Michael was touched. "That she was so taken by this quiet, unassuming piece of furniture in this almost religious way is remarkable. It's not just an object. It's of deep emotional importance to her."

A few years ago, Michael read *A Cabinetmaker's Notebook* by James Krenov, among the world's eminent woodworkers.

Krenov wrote, "Sometimes, when I work, this creeps into the atmosphere: the sense that maybe the wood and the tools are doing, and want to do, something which is beyond me, a part of me, but more than I am." Michael calls that sensation "the poetry of woodworking." It is not such a presumptuous leap. As poet Rita Dove once wrote, "One writes in order to feel: that is the fundamental mover." So, too, for Michael.

When Michael and Karen deliver the library cabinet to my house, they have added black door pulls that are actually tuning pegs for a viola. He likes that they echo the room's black piano; she likes the way they feel between her thumb and forefinger. Oiled and buffed, the cabinet is aflame, rich and warm in transparent reddish shades and tight, lavish grains. The cabinet, Michael says, isn't only a possession that belongs to my wife and me but an extension of who we are. Other people with the same nook, he says, would have chosen a different style or wood, objected to the bark fingerprint or the viola pegs. Then he stands back, ever confounded.

"I'm very proud of it," he says. "It's beautiful."

TWO

CHARLIE KELLER

THE SCHOLARLY BLACKSMITH

Charlie Keller is dancing between thinking and doing. That's how he imagines his work as he takes up an iron poker and stokes the fire he has just built from soft Pennsylvania coal. The flames gently rise a foot, and the piece of iron he has put in the fire glows at 1,100 degrees Fahrenheit. He knows the temperature because the iron is blood red. When he switches on the forge's blower, the flames lick higher and arc toward the mouth of the chimney. In the next few minutes, as Charlie readies his tools, the iron in the forge runs through the spectrum that acts as a blacksmith's thermometer.

> Blood red: 1,100 degrees.
> Dark cherry: 1,300 degrees.
> Orange: 1,800 degrees.
> Light yellow: 2,300 degrees.
> Dazzling white: 3,000 degrees.

When hot iron turns the color of dark cherry, the metal is soft enough to reshape with a hammer. At light yellow, it goes slick – resembling a glowing ice cube – and is ready to forge-weld. At dazzling white, it begins to decompose and flares like a Fourth of July sparkler. Charlie knows what iron will do at each color as he forges replicas of colonial hoes, spades and rakes; ladles, hasps and potato hooks; and, the tool he is making today for a New Zealand museum, a Kentucky ax. Without giving it much thought, he reads the fire thermometer. This morning, at light cherry, he will hammer indentations where the Kentucky ax handle goes. When the ax head glows orange, he will remove it and pound it 30 times on his anvil with a 2 1/2-pound hammer to begin forging a cutting edge. When the luminescence of the ax dulls, Charlie will feel the hammer hitting more solid iron and will hear its concussion clanging at a higher pitch. Then he will know it is time to stop and plunge the ax back into the flames.

He will do these things as instinctively as a speed skater crouching more deeply at the hint of a head wind. No analysis, all sensation, with mechanics and intuition layered upon each other seamlessly. In the way that, away from the rink, a skater could calculate the physics of wind resistance, Charlie could check hot iron's exact Fahrenheit readings by turning to a chart in his book *Cognition and Tool Use: The Blacksmith at Work*, coauthored with his wife, anthropologist Janet Dixon Keller of the University of Illinois at Urbana-Champaign.

But he doesn't. In his blacksmith shop in rural Newman, Illinois, the exact temperatures on that chart might as well be written in a foreign language. It is the language of fire – and the language of experience, imagery, motion, weight, balance, sound, sight and feel – that a blacksmith must read. Years ago, Charlie was only a reader of words, a professor of anthropology. His curiosity slowly pulled him into the world of craftsmanship, where ideas can't be distinguished from objects, thought can't be distinguished from labor – doing is thinking. Today, his life-work is to help the millions of us who no longer make objects with our hands appreciate the few of us who still do.

"Humans are makers," says Charlie, a short, rounding, muscular 61-year-old with a graying beard and rough, thick hands. This morning as he works at the forge, smoke swirls in beams of sunlight that shoot through his dim shop's few windows. The iron in the fire smells like a cast-iron skillet that's been on a hot stove too long. "We have forgotten that, for two and a half million years, everyone made things," he says. Sometimes, when Charlie is listening to an academic colleague argue that a craftsman shapes, say, a ladle as he does because its dipping function requires its bowl-like form, he can only shake his head. His chattering colleague usually has no idea how many hundreds of choices and millions of tiny experiences go into the hand-making of even a simple ladle. *Yeah*, Charlie will think to himself as the man speaks, *come out to the shop, and I'll give you a hammer.*

Charlie was a California boy who was going to be a trombone player, until he took an archaeology class in college. He got hooked. He earned his doctorate from the University of California at Berkeley and excavated African sites where people had made stone tools 400,000 years ago. His crew's dirt picks kept dulling, so he hired a Tanzanian blacksmith to forge them sharp. For hours on end, Charlie found himself watching the old man, wondering exactly how the man—how all craftsmen—*thought* about their work.

He was always handy. As a boy, he built model sailboats. As a teen, he rebuilt a '31 Ford. As a man, he worked on his own house, even re-roofed it. He loved solving the little problems of workmanship, figuring out just how to file the curve of a sailboat's wooden bow so it would slice through the waves, how to set the old Ford's carburetor to spit just the right mouthful of gas, how to calculate the rows of shingles so they'd end up hanging the correct 3/8 inch over the roof's edge. But he also loved the doing: laying row after row of shingles, the aching in his hammer arm, the smell of tar and sweat, his left hand reaching for a shingle, his fingertips feeling its tacky warmth from the hot sun, sliding the shingle into place, reaching for a nail held in his mouth and pounding the nail in with three dead-on hammer blows. And doing it again, again and again. It was beyond ideas and words.

Yet he knew that to many intellectuals, physical labor is equivalent to the force that machines bring to bear on a job – blind, brute power. Charlie believed otherwise: Physical labor wasn't akin to dumb force but was a kind of intelligence. People often thought that a craftsman was closer to a draft animal than to a thinker, he suspected, because they didn't understand the amazing coordination of human senses that accomplishes the work. But he figured there was only one way to unravel the mysteries of thinking and doing.

"I needed to be taught something real," he says.

So 23 years ago, Charlie decided to learn a craft. Remembering his fascination with the Tanzanian blacksmith, he moved to Santa Fe, New Mexico, and apprenticed himself to two blacksmiths. He cleaned floors, painted walls, lugged iron – and struggled to learn blacksmithing, which to an observer looks awfully simple: heat, hammer, bend.

One day, Charlie was trying to read the temperature of a piece of hot iron, hold it with tongs in his left hand and turn it like a slab of meat to heat it evenly, use his right hand to adjust the amount of coal he needed, make certain that ashes weren't building up in the firebox and cooling the fire, watch for the iron to turn light cherry at 1,600 degrees so he knew it had reached forging temperature, figure out what tool he was going to use to shape the iron once he pulled it from the flames. No doubt, he was looking as awkward as a gritty nail-banger in a philosophy class when one of his mentors, standing in the shop, calmly smoking a cigarette, said, "Think hot."

Think hot? What the hell did that mean?

In time, the admonition revealed its meaning. A blacksmith must think as if he were his material, as if his material were, well, alive. He must accept the nature of iron and fire and tools – and think as they would, if they could. "Think hot" was practical and metaphorical advice, akin to a music teacher telling a student to relax and enter the music or a veteran race-car driver telling a novice to let the car drive itself. The suggestions mean nothing at first, seem loony. But in those who will someday be the best musicians, race-car drivers and craftsmen, the advice poses a mental and emotional stance toward *doing* that is beyond words.

That day, though, Charlie was a long way from beyond anything. He first had to learn that to get the right striking angle he must stand square to his anvil with his feet in a baseball batter's stance; that to thin, thicken, lengthen, narrow or spread hot iron he must use a metal hammer, but to straighten twisted iron he must use a wooden mallet; that the forge's firebox must be large enough to allow most of the oxygen to be consumed, or oxidation will pit the iron; that a 1/2-inch-thick iron bar heated to 2,500 degrees stays hot enough to forge for only 60 seconds; that when punching a hole in hot iron, he must feel the first strike when the punch no longer indents the iron because an extra hammer blow will bury the punch in cold iron, like King Arthur's sword in the stone; and that when iron reaches forge-welding temperature it erupts in almost imperceptible sparks. And those were mere details.

In his head, Charlie had to learn to create a picture of the object he hoped to make and then to imagine all the steps between. This imagery, as he came to call it, demanded not only experience but retrospective knowledge: the ability to look at finished objects by other craftsmen and to work backward to unravel the steps taken to make those pieces. From this, he learned the unspoken value blacksmiths share: Made objects should look as if they grew that way. So they must be forged hot in 60-second intervals, because cold-hammered iron looks stiff and lifeless. The revelation to Charlie was that blacksmiths don't revere their final objects – they revere what a man must know and master to be able to make the objects. As much as any intellectual, they revere knowledge.

"It's knowing for doing," he says.

People often think of craftsmen as commonsensical mechanics whose skills grow from dexterity, patience and repetition. Charlie came to reject that idea. "Craftsmanship is not common sense. What craftsmen do isn't intuition. It is hardlearned and complex and visual and intellectual. Always, there's a risk of failure. That's the rush."

Over the years, Charlie came to understand why craftsmen are often so bad at describing how they work. "They aren't verbal because the knowledge isn't verbal." Could Charlie Parker have put his saxophone playing into words? Could Laurence Olivier have explained how he became Hamlet? Could Janet Evans elucidate what happened when she hit the water? Charlie discovered that competitive swimmers move more slowly when they think too much about stroke mechanics. Musicians play worse. Performers act stiffly.

"A lot of mental people really do think manual labor is of a lower order," he says. "But labor isn't just the means to the thrill of being done. There is satisfaction to the labor itself. Passion for the work grows from the feeling you get doing the work." He compares it to the runner's high. "I'm saying that the tactile, visual and physical are as important to developing intelligence as language and that this intelligence is acquired from interacting with objects. This carries profound implications for a society where we no longer produce anything."

Finally, after 15 years of blacksmithing as research, Charlie committed the anthropologist's greatest sin – he went native. He quit university teaching and bought a share of an 1870 blacksmith shop that was being used for storage. Today, his tool replicas are in museums and at living-history sites in more than two dozen states and several countries. His tools appear in the film of *The Last of the Mohicans*. A few years ago, *Early American Life Magazine* named him one of the finest 200 traditional craftsmen in the United States. Yet, at night, he still writes academic articles about the mind of the craftsman.

"I want the thoughtfulness of these men recognized."

By the end of the workday, Charlie is drenched in sweat. The temperature at the forge can rise to 130 degrees. Today, he has put the pieces of his Kentucky ax head in the fire and taken them out again probably a hundred times, forge-welded them together and hammered out the rough shape of a cutting edge. He has swung his hammer maybe a thousand times. He's tired and filthy. Grime is caked under his nails, and muck outlines the wrinkles on his neck. He wipes a streak of ash from his forehead. Charlie looks at himself and laughs.

"That's why philosophers don't want to deal with this stuff. It's too dirty."

THREE

SAM MALOOF

A WOODWORKER'S WORLD

Sam Maloof made a world. In a citrus grove now surrounded by malls and houses, in a wood shop where he handbuilt furniture that is now revered as art, in the home he crafted one room at a time as he could afford the lumber and where he has lived the last half century, almost every minute of every day, with the wonder of his life – his wife, Alfreda – Sam Maloof made a world. He nurtured his lemons and oranges and figs, planted walnut and sycamore trees that started as cuttings the size of his thumb and eventually grew to engulf the grounds. He tore down a chicken coop and built a shop that always smells of sweet, fresh wood. He tore down a shack and built a house that, like a piece of modern sculpture, has no front or back. In the kitchen, he laid bricks without mortar so that each step makes the music of wind chimes. Then he moved on to the living room, Freda's study, the sky-lit tower, the guest room with a loft, the balcony overlooking the grove. The house ultimately came to 7,000 square feet – 26 rooms that unfold like a pyramid's secret chambers adorned with handmade redwood doors, windows and jalousies, two dozen wooden door latches that resemble flying fish or bones or tusks, jagged-edged walnut dog-boards nailed to the wall like abstract art, Douglas fir rafters with mortise-and-tenon joints at their peaks, window frames joined with dovetails, even toilet seats handmade from English oak and black walnut. Outside the grove, cars and trucks groan and spew and honk in stagnant air while, inside the grove, birds are always singing and a breeze is always rustling the trees. The question everyone wants answered is: Would Sam Maloof's craftsman genius have blossomed if he had not first created this world in which to live and work? In other words, did his genius create this place, or did this place create his genius?

"Oh, I don't know," Sam says. "What do you think, Freda?"

Sam and Freda are puttering around their house in Alta Loma, California, at the foot of the San Gabriel Mountains.

She is tidying the kitchen. He is giving a tour of the house and the 100 handmade chairs and tables, desks and settees, coffee tables, beds and dressers that decorate it, of the woodshop, of the six acres of lemons, peaches, pears, apricots, figs and avocados that sit like an island in a sprawling suburban sea. But this island, like Atlantis, is about to disappear forever, to be buried not underwater but under concrete, a new section of the nearby Foothill Freeway. Because Sam's house and workshop are on the National Register of Historic Places, they will be moved to a scraggly citrus grove nearby and turned into a working museum. He will design a new house on the new grounds for himself and Freda.

"It's sort of scary sometimes," he says of his success and fame, which have seemed almost to overtake him in recent years. His furniture is in the Metropolitan Museum of Art, the Smithsonian Institution's Renwick Gallery, the White House and the homes of former presidents Jimmy Carter and Ronald Reagan. A dining room set he sold for $3,000 about 25 years ago resold recently for $150,000. One of his new high-backed rockers today sells for $18,000. Sam is hailed today not as a furniture maker but as an artist. Yet for all his success, Sam, at 82, is too militantly modest to take credit. And Freda, at 86, is too down-to-earth to think Sam – or anyone, for that matter – can deserve the world-renowned stature he has achieved.

"God's been very good to us," Freda says.

"I'd say I was lucky," Sam says, "but I worked doggone hard."

Freda flashes an ironic smile. "I didn't know he was going to be so famous."

Sam is embarrassed. "Oh, Freda."

"Freda helped me," Sam says. Fifty years ago he was working as a graphic artist for a California company that made decals, but he wanted to quit and make furniture for a living. "She didn't say, 'You're crazy. Just stay where you are. At least you're making a living.' She said, 'If you want to do it, I think you should do it.'" After Sam lost money on his first commissioned pieces of furniture, he told Freda he was going back to graphics. She said, "No, you can do it."

"You talk about faith, hope and charity," Sam says. "She had it for me. I would have given up if it hadn't been for Freda."

"I was just happy he was doing something he loved," Freda says.

Doing what Sam loved – creating about 50 pieces of furniture a year for 50 years – has made him one of the most respected craftsmen in the country. His chairs have the curving grace of a parabola, the embracing comfort of loving arms and the tactile sensuality of supple skin. They look and feel like living creatures, not pieces of wood connected by dowel and glue and joint, but single, seamless waves of wood. Sam once watched as the blind bluesman Ray Charles caressed a piece of his furniture and announced that it had "soul." Sam likes that story because soul is a place beyond words, where hand, head and humanity blur.

"You can't have soul without sincerity," he says.

Sam and Freda are short and silver-haired. She is lithe and fragile and walks with an airy glide, her silky hair tucked up in a little twist. She speaks so softly that the last words of her sentences, like a distant sound trailing off, can be lost. She has a mild laugh, more like a sigh. And that ironic smile. Sam, on the other hand, is compact and muscular, nothing fragile about him. He walks with the spring of an athlete. He speaks slowly but with a deep voice that's always audible. He looks a decade younger than his years, easy. Freda has always kept Sam grounded. Early in his career, when art-show judges rejected two pieces of Sam's work, he hang-dogged around the house looking for sympathy.

"Sam," Freda said, "rejection is good for the ego."

Decades later, when he won a $375,000 MacArthur Foundation "genius" grant, he was embarrassed at the ceremony that other winners' résumés went on and on with various accomplishments and advanced degrees. His read: "Sam Maloof, Chino High School graduate, 1934, designer." Freda just flashed her smile: "Sam, I bet there isn't a person here who knows how to make a chair." And when President Jimmy Carter and First Lady Rosalynn, who own several pieces of Sam's furniture, stopped by the lemon grove one day, it was Freda who calmly asked the Carters to stay for dinner.

"She cooked chicken casserole," Sam says.

Freda shrugs. "Well, that's what we would have eaten."

"And he," Sam says of President Carter, "had two helpings."

Freda believes Sam could write a book about the famous people he has met.

"No," says Sam, suddenly serious. "A memoir: How I met and married you."

Now Freda is embarrassed. "Oh, Sam."

Sam's workshop connects to the house through an alcove off the living room. A giant fan sucks a cool breeze into the long, high-roofed building. Chairs are everywhere – half built, built, unsanded, sanded, unfinished, finished. Eight will go to a CEO in the Napa Valley. One will go to Singapore. Two to Atlanta. Each takes about a week of Sam's cutting, shaping and gluing. Sam and three workers will then sand and finish them. Freda will send the bills and enter the sales in the books. Wooden templates marked with the names of the first people to buy each style of chair – Miller, Evans, Mars, Hafif—hang like stalactites from the ceiling. Hulking around the room are joiners, lathes, a planer, a band saw, a drill press, a shaper and a spindle sander. And holstered in a wooden rack along the wall are chisels – Sam's favorite is 50 years old and has been sharpened down to a 1-inch nub.

"It's like a favorite cup," he says. "You get used to it."

Sam still works 60 hours a week in the shop, down from the 80, 90 or 100 he worked as a younger man scratching out a living. Now almost every day, after he and Freda eat the lunch she has made, he takes a nap. Freda insists. She had not been well lately, and that has worried Sam. Their son, Slimen, also a woodworker, had never seen his father so pensive and distracted, so unable to concentrate, as when Freda was sick.

"What'd the doctor say," Sam asks Freda when she pokes her head into the workshop after returning from a morning checkup.

"I'm fine."

"I'm sure glad you're OK," he says as Freda heads back into the house.

He is quiet for a moment, still looking worried about Freda. Finally, he goes on with his conversation. "The way people react to my furniture," he says, "it's almost embarrassing." He gets letters by the hundreds – the woodworker who says meeting Sam briefly more than a decade ago changed his life, the composer who studies Sam's furniture as inspiration for his music, the woman who says that every time she looks closely at Sam's chair in her living room she cries at its beauty. Sam is human. He likes the respect that borders on adulation. But it baffles him.

"I went into woodworking thinking it would be a nice way of making a living," he says. He wasn't thinking about becoming famous or rich or making a chair that would be enshrined in the Smithsonian. He just couldn't imagine commuting to an office cubicle. Yet now people study Sam to understand how the way he lives his life has fostered his creativity. He tells the curious that creativity is inherent in humans, God-given, although it can be either nurtured or suppressed. And blind determination matters. Sam has known craftsmen who worked hard for short periods and found that no one would buy their furniture. Their feelings hurt, they quit. He has known woodworkers who believed they deserved recognition after making only a few pieces. He has known furniture makers who sold their designs to production companies, took the money and never built another piece. He believes that affirmation, glory and wealth are motivators that will do little to create a fine craftsman.

"You do it because of the love," he says.

In his shop this morning, Sam is working for himself. Forty-five years ago, he made a chair for Freda's mother, now dead. He has looked at that chair with his perfectionist eye for years, thinking the back is too small for its body and that he should fix it someday. Today is the day. He has taken a 2 1/2-by-4-by-16-inch chunk of walnut in his hands and begun to sculpt it on the band saw, trimming away much of its thickness into a curving wave along what will be the new back of the chair. As he usually does, Sam stops what he's doing to work on another chair for awhile, turning a leg on the lathe. Reddish walnut flecks mist his hair, eyebrows and arms.

"You have to feel it," Sam says of the work. "You make a joint that fits absolutely perfectly, and you feel it. I still pinch myself. I'm not a workaholic. I just enjoy my work." Never has Sam had a day when he woke up and didn't feel the desire to work. "Sometimes the day is gone before I get started," he says. He wonders: What if he had opened a workshop somewhere in an industrial zone, commuted there every morning, commuted home every night? Would he have made the furniture he did? He thinks not.

This world – this shop, this house, the grove, Freda, his daughter, who grew up here running in and out of the shop, his son, who became a woodworker in the grove, the men who have been with him for decades – this world created Sam as much as Sam created it. He is a meticulous man, who painstakingly laid the stones at his house's entryway to look as if they were scattered at random. Everything here is as if Sam took a pencil and drew this world, then entered it. With stones laid, fig trees, olive cuttings and sycamore saplings carefully planted, woodwork covering nearly every square inch of the house. Like a poet who writes a line and then must respond to that now existing line in the next sentence, Sam was shaped by the world he shaped. His creativity, he believes, is rooted here in the grove, in the house, in the workshop. Freda is back, standing at the door, waiting for the lathe to wind down.

"What's up?" Sam asks.

"Seth died yesterday afternoon."

"Seth died?" He was a friend from their Methodist church.

"He died."

"I saw him yesterday. He was fine."

"He was in the garden, and he fell over dead."

"Oh, my God! This is a sad thing."

Sam goes back to turning, clearing his mind as he presses a gouge into the narrowing bottom of the chair leg. Wood mist flies again. "That's the way to go," he finally says – in the garden, doing what you love. "People say, 'Work must be the most important thing in your life,' and I say, 'But it isn't. First comes God, then my family, my friends, my work, in that order.' Without my family and friends, I would have no interest in work."

That sentiment, beyond furniture, is really what has made Sam Maloof famous, as he and Freda have become a moral lesson on what so many people fear is missing in their lives. Sam and Freda left the bureaucratic, workaday world to live in a citrus grove beyond callous civilization. Sam never advertised. He once turned down an offer worth $22 million to mass-produce department-store versions of his furniture. People came to him by word of mouth, like disciples. He labored day and night in his work-sanctified shop, and they came to him. Life for Sam and Freda became like a piece of Sam's furniture –organic and seamless: he and Freda walking the misty lemon grove before breakfast, she stopping by the shop on hot afternoons with lemonade, the two of them cooking dinner at night for raw-handed woodworkers, CEOs, even a President. So what is the secret to creative work?

Sam tells this story: He once sent a friend's son looking for a summer job to the famous Pennsylvania woodworker George Nakashima. The boy later called Sam and told him that Nakashima had hung up on him. Sam asked the boy what had been said.

Nakashima: "I couldn't teach you to sweep my floors in three months."

Boy: "I know how to sweep floors."

At that answer, Nakashima had hung up.

The correct answer: "If it takes a year, I want to learn to do it."

"I would have hung up on him also," Sam says. "There has to be a humility."

The men who work with Sam are master craftsmen, but sometimes for weeks they do nothing but sand spindles. "But they wouldn't even think of doing a poor job because they were bored," Sam says. "It isn't because of how much I pay them. They do it for themselves. You have to work with integrity."

To be a fine craftsman, Sam believes, you must first be a good person. Somehow the qualities that make good people – humility, patience, integrity, sincerity – transfer to the objects a person makes. To Sam, that is a gift passed from God. After all, what is God if not goodness living in the hearts and minds and creations of people? Sam says he can teach anyone to be a good woodworker. But a person can't be a fine woodworker without a good heart, and that, he cannot teach. "You have to be able to see the beauty around you," Sam says.

Once he and Freda were walking through the woods, stopping to look at how a leaf was shaped or a stem held its flower. "And then Freda saw a little bird's nest. It was abandoned. It was so beautiful. To see how a tiny bird could create and build such a beautiful nest is amazing to me. Life is discovery." They took the nest home and still have it on a shelf. Each time Sam and Freda notice it, they are transported back to that day in the woods.

It will be hard for Sam and Freda to leave this made world. That bird's nest, the flying-fish door latches, the dovetailed redwood window frames, the peaked Douglas fir rafters will all go with them. So, too, will the 100 pieces of Sam's furniture – the chairs, tables, desks, settees, beds and dressers, the rosewood music stand Sam made for violist Jan Hlinka, who willed it back to Sam when he died. And, of course, the piece Freda is now touching gently with her fingertips, that smile on her face.

"This is my rocking chair," she says. "He gave it to me. It has my name on it."

Made for Alfreda Maloof, Christmas, '72. P.S. All my love.

"It all belongs to Freda," Sam says, motioning to everything around him.

Yet much will stay behind – the sycamore tree Sam planted as a sapling that is now a giant tree, the dry dirt that compresses under his boots on morning walks, the dust that rises with each step, the sunlight as it filters into Freda's study. These pieces of Sam's world can't be moved. But he will not be depressed. "Freda and I have the chance to start life over again," he says. Sam has plans. He will rejuvenate the scraggly citrus grove on his new land. He will plant walnut and maple saplings that will be giant in hope. He will build a Japanese teahouse over the land's arroyo. And he will build a new house.

"The house," he says, "will be like a piece of furniture."

Sam Maloof is again about to make a world.

The question still: Will he create that place, or will that place create him?

"Well," Sam says, "you can't have one without the other."

FOUR

BOB DIX

TIME THROUGH A KEYHOLE

ate at night, as ever, Bob Dix is hunched over a long workbench in a small room in a corner of his basement. A white cloth, unfolded before him, is the soft bed for a palm-size, battered, filthy and lifeless padlock built by hand during the Civil War. Bob is a bear of a man with a strong, resounding voice and manner, but he handles his artifact with the delicacy of a jeweler. He leans to his work, Mozart's K.424 Duo in B-Flat for violin and viola floating lightly in the air, an otoscope his father the doctor used 50 years ago held to his right eye, the lock lifted to within inches. The lock is four and a half inches long, three inches wide, half an inch deep and weighs eight ounces. Its shape is reminiscent of a Valentine's Day heart or, for the less romantic, a heel that has fallen off a big man's boot. It has the coarse touch of sandpaper. But through the looking glass, the microscopic asperities of this corroded brass lock become for Bob Dix a panorama of historical imaginings.

"Boy, this is classic fire damage," he says. "It was hanging on a door and the building caught fire. Something fell on it, and the key broke off and the case got wrinkled in the pressure and the heat. I think that's the whole scenario. Thank God it didn't melt. Maybe it was in the Civil War. Maybe it was buried and dug out later. Heaven only knows."

The lock is returned to its bed, the otoscope laid aside. The 51-year-old man, who is one of the finest locksmiths in the United States, straightens in his chair, purses his lips and raises his brow, taking a moment to savor what he is about to do. "This lock hasn't been opened in nearly a hundred and fifty years. It's like opening an Egyptian tomb." One of Bob's friends bought the lock – unworkable and with its key broken off in the keyhole – in a New Orleans antique shop. Stamped on the shackle was "S. Andrews," revealing it had been built in the Perth Amboy, New Jersey, locksmith shop of Solomon Andrews. The friend paid $40. When Bob Dix is done, some collector will likely buy this one-of-a-kind relic for $1,200 – 30 times its cost.

Bob reaches for a miniature drill, bit size .07, stations it above the first of nine 3/16-inch-wide rivets that secure the lock's case, then fingers and releases the trigger and lowers the drill, letting it bite into the rivet's head only on the down side of the motor's whining run. If the bit were to slip off the rounded rivet with the drill under power, it would mine a twirl of brass from the case, which would leave a gouge another locksmith, another traveler in this niche of human history, might someday ponder in the way Bob ponders just how this padlock came to be damaged in a fire. He unfurls his arms like an orchestra conductor and motions to walls that are the backdrop for a cavernous art gallery of locks, some glinting bright brass and steel, others hanging dull and ashen, locks 2,000 years old, locks still in the factory wrap.

"Everything here is a story," he says.

Seven thousand stories are stored in Bob's Mentor, Ohio, basement, which houses probably the world's largest collection of locks. Each reveals a sliver of history. A lock from the Dark Ages is made in the unadorned, utilitarian style of the era. A later lock, beautifully etched, shows the emerging artistry of the Renaissance. The simple mechanisms of antique European locks contrast with the intricate, clockmaker styles of 19th-century American locksmiths. The 1,100 "logo locks" include the trade names of business giants long dead to altered times: Hudson Motor Car Co., Cadillac Cleveland Tank, Belle Isle Creamery. And the pride of the collection: the signed O.L. Stacy lock Bob believes was the first pin tumbler ever built and the precursor to the revolutionary line of locks launched in the 19th century by Linus Yale Jr. The pin tumbler allowed infinite master keying and made possible the billions of locks that today secure houses, cars, hotel rooms and offices.

"Locks are talking to you," Bob says, as he gigs his drill again and it whines, digging into another rivet. "They are living pieces of history." When the drill stops, he sweeps away the brass chaff with his finger and examines his work through the otoscope. "Okay, that one's good."

Solomon Andrews was a New Jersey dentist who also made locks. Bob has smaller Andrews locks, strong steel locks, good locks. This brass lock was cheap, made for an emerging mass market. Bob knows that the men who made this junk lock would think him crazy for spending 30 hours restoring it. But to him, it's like a cracked dish unearthed from a vanished culture. He'll restore it, as he has thousands of others, not for the money but so it will not disappear. He shakes the lock and it rains rust.

"What's coming out is making me nervous. I don't know how much mechanism is left. The important thing is the levers. Do I have to make the levers? I will if they lost too much strength in the fire. I'm really anxious to see what's inside. I have never heard of anyone finding an original Solomon Andrews key."

Bob was eight when his grandmother bought him his first lock, an inexpensive Slaymaker. Bob took it apart and put it back together. He was always taking things apart – radios, TVs, telephones, the family clocks. By the time he was 12, he'd go shopping with his mother in downtown Cleveland, and she'd drop him off at the locksmith shop of "old man Sackman," who'd let young Bob work on simple locks. He began collecting locks. After college, he took a job with Lubrizol Corp., the giant petroleum-additive company near Cleveland. He has worked there 29 years and today is in charge of automating the company's testing labs. All those years, night after night, he has gone down to his basement cavern and unfolded his white cloth.

"Hmm, which rivet is holding it?" he asks, as he lightly squeezes the handles of the reverse-pressure pliers he has inserted inside the edge of the Andrews lock, where the shackle's toe enters, hoping to loosen its front from its back. He has drilled his tiny holes in the rivets that hold the front and the back of the case together, because he wants to save as many rivets as he can. If they are sturdy enough, he'll later insert a tiny screw in the top of each one. The screw-turns will snap off with pressure and leave a protruding tip atop the rivet that he will then round off to perfectly match the exterior tip of the original rivets. After drilling his holes, Bob files off the rivets' rounded tops, leaving only a leaf-thin lip to hold them in place. Then, with a tiny jeweler's screwdriver, he chisels off the lips, leaving nothing but corrosion to hold the case together. "Let's put a nice, even force." He gently squeezes his pliers—pop. "Not since the Civil War," he whispers, and lifts off the lid of the tomb. "Oh, my goodness. There's the mechanism."

He does a quick inventory. Four, maybe five of the nine rivets are rusted beyond redemption. The lock was definitely in a fire, its back distorted from melting. But it wasn't buried, no dirt. The remnant of the lock's broken key is brass, meaning it could be the original key, the first Solomon Andrews key he has ever discovered. Strange, but the leading edge of the key was cut at a 30-degree angle, something Bob has never seen. The lock's works are ingeniously simple: four wishbone springs that served as both levers and bolts, supplying pressure to open the lock and pressure to close it. But Bob can't yet tell how it worked.

"I have to sit here and figure it out."

Never has Bob touched a lock he hasn't figured out. He can put his lock-picking tools in a keyhole, and in a matter of moments the lock is open. After 43 years of working with locks, he actually visualizes how the mechanism must be built to fit into a certain size case. He can feel the tumbler's language through his fingertips. He once opened a pair of Houdini handcuffs in 20 minutes. He once rebuilt a famous 150-year-old F. Harn trick lock that had lost its entire innards. He stared at that empty lock – a puzzle frame without pieces – for three years. One day, in a flash, he saw the only combination of space and mechanism that would fit. The collector for whom he was rebuilding the lock refused to take it back, so awed was he by the achievement.

"It's your lock now," he said.

Bob doesn't just sit down and do these things. He'll carry a lock in his pocket for days or weeks, take it out and flip it in his hand while studying a computer program at work or watching the History Channel at home. He doesn't think about opening the lock. He lets what he calls his subconscious mull the answer. "It's like it comes in a waking dream." He once left an antique Pyes lock, a lock nearly impossible to pick, sitting on his workbench for six months. Then, as he was watching a movie with his wife, he had an urge to go look at the lock. He walked downstairs, opened it in 10 seconds and returned to the movie.

"I hadn't been able to open it before, and I bet I couldn't open it now. It was very strange." He laughs uncomfortably. "The Zen, if you will. It's like, well, you're at another plane with this lock, which sounds crazy for somebody in chemistry and computer science to say. But I see it. There are times I fit a key, and I know where to make the cuts in that key, and I can't explain how I know. It's got to be coming from experience and intuition. But it's strange. I lose track of time. My wife gets mad at me. It can be two or three in the morning, I don't even know it. Unless you experience it, it's hard to describe. If you try to talk to somebody who doesn't understand, they think you're nuts. You don't talk about the state of mind you need to be in to do this work."

It's the same state of mind he believes the best people in any field must also reach. The greatest musicians aren't only technically proficient, Bob knows, but also reach an intuitive plane with their music. So too great athletes, actors, writers, artists—but also scientists. Einstein knew the same *facts* as other physicists, but he looked at the puzzle's empty frame and saw the only way the pieces of time, space and matter could fit. "It's a mind-set," Bob says. Craftsmen – supposedly simple, practical, hands-on people – are thought to be outside this intuitive realm, but Bob knows they are not. "It's spooky stuff, but that's how it goes."

Jean-Marie Ledair's Sonata, Op. 3, No. 4 in F is floating lightly in the air. Bob has for hours now soaked the pieces of the Andrews lock in an ultrasonic bath that creates millions of tiny exploding bubbles that clean the corrosion. He has polished the case and shackle to a burnished antique brass, giving it the smooth feel of a waxed oak plank. With tweezers, he has carefully removed the lever bolts, all but three of the rivets and the broken end of the only known Solomon Andrews key in existence. He has decided he may need to anneal—heat, hammer and cool, again and again, a metal piece to find its original shape—the levers to re-impart spring action lost to the fire, but he won't need to make new ones, which is a relief. He has spent hours gently tapping the back of the lock's case between a brass hammer and a brass drift, encouraging the case to take its original form, forget its fire-induced wrinkles.

In this lock, Bob has begun to discern a story. He has decided the lock was an early effort to build a cheap, profitable mass-market product that was doomed from the start. "It was really a crummy lock," he says. The unusual 30-degree cut on the leading edge of the key probably was an effort to compensate for a design flaw in the lock mechanism that would have kept it from opening with a standard key. Bob imagines Andrews saying, "What are we gonna do?" For the locksmith whose intuition flashed on the angled cut, Bob has great respect. But he suspects this faulty lock design was quickly abandoned.

Bob has yet to put the puzzle's pieces back in their frame. He must first make the new rivets on his lathe, cut a new key from the angled artifact and chemically treat the lock to create a deep brown patina that will evoke an elegantly aged character respectful of its antiquity. Then Bob Dix will perform one final act before he closes the case for good: He will etch his name inside the lock of Solomon Andrews and become forever a piece of its story.

FIVE

CHUCK CRISPIN

A PHILOSOPHER
OF EXACTITUDE

huck Crispin is on his knees on the cold concrete, resting back on his haunches, something he tries to remember never to do anymore. At age 45, a hardwood-floor man must treat his knees gently. He's in the Oakwood Inn's library, a small room in the shape of half an octagon. Well, not exactly half an octagon, which is his dilemma. One wall runs five inches longer than the facing wall. One wall has 24-inch bookshelves extending from it, while its opposite has no shelves. That difference has made the room's fireplace look off center. And because the Syracuse, Indiana, lakeside resort hotel is a commercial building, the library's doors swing out for safety, meaning the six inches of red-oak floor that Chuck wants outside his elaborate, laser-carved oak-leaf border will have to be widened along that wall. Otherwise, people inside the library will see carpet poking under the closed doors.

"I am not going to let that happen," he says.

It's after dark, and the spindly lamps he has set around the room cast ghostly shadows. The other workmen were gone and the front doors locked by the time Chuck arrived. At night he doesn't have to hear the booming country music endemic to construction sites these days. He prefers the jazz of Chet Baker or even recorded readings of Shakespeare's sonnets. An hour after he arrives, his brown hair is flecked with oak spalts that spew like sparkler beams from his miter saw as he cuts lengths of flooring. In jeans, penny loafers and a ratty green sweater, his glasses pushed up on his head, Chuck looks more like the disheveled philosophy professor he might have become after graduating from Northwestern University than he does one of America's finest inlaid-floor craftsmen.

"Boy, that is a shame," he finally says, rising from the floor, running stretched fingers through his hair and launching a storm of burnished oak flakes around his head. "I have an asymmetry here that's never going to be perfect. The Greeks spent a lot of time thinking about the correspondence between the ideal and the real. Everything that exists is imperfect. You create the illusion of perfection."

In Chuck's case, that illusion is convincing. Snaking around him on the library floor is an elaborate oak-leaf border of acorns, stems and leaves in 15 colors created in 15 woods from all over the world. The verawood in the acorns is a dark green, and the caps are the deep orange of cumaru. The border's 120 leaves are radiant, with blood-wood, wenge, pau amarillo, American walnut, Brazilian cherry, makore, African mahogany, American cherry, tulipwood, peroba rosa, chakte-kok, cocobolo and purpleheart catching the stark light and glimmering in all the natural shades of a forest. Ten years ago, the border would have been impossible to craft. But today's computer-driven laser beams allow complex designs – oak leaves, roses, trains, anything really – to be cut and placed like pieces of a jigsaw puzzle into a wood floor.

Laser inlays aren't for the weak of wallet. Chuck charges $12.50 a square foot for a standard red-oak floor. For a classic parquet pattern – a Monticello or a Bordeaux – it's $20. For the library floor, he's charging $30 a square foot. The 4.5-inch-wide border alone costs $75 a linear foot – or $4,800 of the job's $8,000 price tag. When the laser revolution was just coming ashore, Chuck and his tiny Legendary Hardwood Floors in his hometown of Terre Haute, Indiana, jumped on the first wave. But technology hasn't changed the way he sees his craft. In the everyday world of workmen, he's a rarity – a devotee of T.S. Eliot and Søren Kierkegaard, of Gabriel Garcia Marquez and Milan Kundera.

"I tried to be a philosopher and it just wasn't in me," he says. After earning his bachelor's degree in philosophy (with a minor in classics), Chuck just couldn't stomach the idea of more school, nor could he imagine himself ever working in, say, an insurance agency. "Not anything having to do with a bureaucracy."

Chuck was a free spirit. For two years, he worked in a foundry and saved money. Then he bounced around Europe for a few years, part of the time as a groundskeeper at an estate in Luxembourg with a 17th-century castle. When he returned to Terre Haute, he got married and had a daughter and a son. But with a degree in philosophy, he was virtually unemployable. So he began a small contracting business – decks, bathrooms, siding. It seemed a good choice. "The only thing that ever made me feel real was working with my hands," he says. Financially, it was tough. For five years, he went from little job to little job.

"It was a grim life."

One winter when business was even slower than usual, Chuck refinished a friend's wood floor, a job he'd never done. "It was like changing water to wine," he says. "I was so fascinated, I couldn't wait to do it again." During the next few years, Chuck began to specialize in refinishing floors. Then, a decade ago, Alan Pyne of Brookfield, Wisconsin, hired him to lay a floor in a Terre Haute mansion. Pyne, a taciturn 70-year-old legend among wood floor men, set a standard Chuck hadn't known.

"Cut it again," he told Chuck after he had left a sixteenth-inch space between two boards. The second time Chuck left a thirty-second of an inch. "It's not tight enough," Pyne said. Finally, Chuck cut a piece so it had to be pounded into place. Said Pyne, "That's the way I want it."

The apprentice fell hard for the master's exactitude. "The kick, the endorphin rush, was the thrill you get participating in excellence," Chuck says. To Pyne's mechanical precision, Chuck grafted his own philosophical bent. "I don't want my life's work to be wasted. I want to do something durable. To Wordsworth, that's 'the intimation of immortality.'" Chuck laughs at himself. "We're talking wood floors now. But I'll take whatever little piece of immortality I can get." After learning about laser cutting from Pyne, Chuck began creating his own inlays. As an amateur poet, actor, painter and sculptor, he loved the artistry of designing new patterns, researching exotic woods to figure out which were strong enough, experimenting to find out what colors the woods would be after they were finished.

"It was a way to combine my work and my creativity."

For himself, Chuck made a border in six exotic woods patterned on a design he saw in a St. Louis chapel built by T.S. Eliot's grandfather. For a 5-year-old boy, he created a train border in seven woods based on photos of the cars and locomotive that carried Abraham Lincoln back to Illinois after his death. For a couple who collect Native American artifacts, he crafted an inlay in nine woods that shows two Kokopelli dancers playing their flutes beneath a giant yellow moon.

Over the years, Chuck has inlaid at least 50 exotic woods in floors, including Australian lacewood, Laotian jackwood and New Zealand rewarewa. He has learned through trial and error that snakewood is too dense for the laser. It cuts by burning through wood, which means that dense, oily or overly moist woods that take a long time to cut will be severely burned along their edges or can even burst into flames. He has learned that while American cherry costs $3 a square foot, bloodwood costs $25 a square foot, and African pink ivory is sold not by the square foot but by the ounce, like gold. He has learned that the grain in the leaves of his oak-leaf border should always run outward from the stems to mimic the veins of a real leaf.

Eventually, Chuck learned to ask his clients about their lives. In the floor of one home, he copied the 18th-century marquetry inlay of a favorite antique table, adding roses, tulips and irises in 11 woods. After learning that Garcia Marquez was the favorite novelist of one of his clients, he inlaid the South American lignumvitae wood mentioned in the author's *One Hundred Years of Solitude*. Chuck fears he sounds pretentious, but he has come to think of his custom floors as narratives that echo his clients' lives. "T.S. Eliot says thought is the opposite of action, but I disagree," he says. "Ideas and their execution in reality are inseparable."

Consider the Oakwood Inn's library floor. Chuck walked into the room when its walls were still a skeleton of studs and its concrete floor was littered with construction debris. But he looked around and saw the new floor, the idea for it. That was the exhilarating instant: *I can do this!* Then he saw tainted reality – the walls out of sync, the fireplace off-kilter. So he began calculating how to create the illusion of perfection. He'd center the corners of his oak-leaf border on the room's focal point – the fireplace – instead of on the walls. His ideal six-inch red-oak reveal around the border would be fudged at the doorway, adjusted a quarter-inch along one wall, three-eighths along another. The 22.5-degree turn in the border would be cheated a hair along the wall that's too long. No, it wouldn't be perfect. "But when you walk into this room," Chuck says, "you'll need a tape measure to see it."

To install a wood floor right, there's a lot to know. Chuck dry-lays almost every one of his floors completely to be sure it will fit perfectly. The library's subfloor is concrete, so he decided to use quartersawn red oak that costs $3.80 a square foot compared with $2.40 for plainsawn. In the high-humidity lakeside resort, the quartersawn boards will expand more up and down than across, diminishing ugly gaps and warping.

Before laying the floor, Chuck waited 60 days for the concrete to cure fully, which prevents moisture from seeping into the wood and causing it to warp. At installation in this Midwest climate, the wood must measure 6 to 8 percent moisture to limit gapping. When Chuck glues a floor over concrete, he pushes the tongue of each piece into the groove of the adjacent piece. That keeps the groove from acting like a spoon and collecting glue that then interferes with a tight fit. When laying wood floor over wood subfloor, he reverses the process and pushes groove into tongue, so each exposed tongue can then be nailed to the subfloor.

Nailing matters too. On oak or pine floors, a pneumatic nailer can be used. But on extra-hard woods like Brazilian cherry or cumaru, holes must be drilled in the tongues and nails driven in by hand. Otherwise the tongues will split slightly at each nail, making the floor squeak when people walk on it. Chuck even rips the grooves off pieces of flooring that run along the wall to eliminate weak spots that might crack if something heavy were dropped. Perhaps most important, he routs, slip-tongues and glues all corner-cut pieces to prevent their ends from curling after a decade and to make the entire floor interlock.

Installing the inlays adds more complications. The laser beam, for instance, expands as it cuts through wood, leaving a wider cut at the bottom than at the top. That means Chuck must lather glue more heavily on the inlays than on the rest of the flooring so it will rise up into the cuts and secure the small pieces not only from the bottom but also along the sides. Yet he can't use too much glue or it will seep up through the inlay's seams. Then he must check each piece to be certain it's centered within its cut. To eliminate scratches in the finish, Chuck uses a random-orbit sander. A smooth surface keeps the light-reddish stain he uses to bring out the wood's highlights from soaking in very far, creating a sense of visual depth after two coats of polyurethane are applied. The floor is then buffed glassy with a 180-grit screen over a soft pad, and a final coat of polyurethane is brushed on.

"The entire process is like a song, something complete in itself," he says. He then gives this simple description of crafts-manship: "You get an idea, fiddle with it, make sure the execu-tion measures up to the authenticity of the concept, don't have a failure in materials or workmanship, don't cut corners. A lot of guys have nice ideas, and then they leave an eighth-inch gap in their work."

Pulling up his goggles, studying the cut he has just made, smoothing it with his fingers, he says, "If you're not obsessive, you won't be a craftsman. It's the difference between being a believer and being a fanatic. A believer goes to church and sings hymns and believes he's going to heaven. A fanatic sells his shirt, gives the proceeds to the poor and races off to convert the heathens. A real craftsman has to be a fanatic." He laughs and adds, "The only thing sadder than a dying luxury car is a mediocre craftsman."

Chuck sees guys who make big bucks throwing down "gun-and-run" floors, laying 900 square feet in the time it takes him to lay 40. The money is tempting. "But I see guys who do that and I'm not sure they're happier. To me, there's something essentially, well, spiritual about my work and how it's bound up with character and how it's bound up with my own self-pride. To me, a great hardwood floor is as nice as a great church window. It's Walt Whitman – it's a song of myself." Chuck raises his arms in mock rapture and whispers, "The human choir!"

It's nearly midnight now. Chuck is tired and slouching. He has sorted through a 997-pound pile of flooring, selected the pieces containing the most stunning medullary rays and laid them aside for placement in front of the library's fireplace. He has laid out the pieces of his inlay jigsaw puzzle. Back down on his knees, he leans his weight on the knuckles of his left hand to secure the last of the corner pieces. He taps the tail of the board lightly seven times with his hammer until it's as tight as a cork in a wine bottle, then forgets his knees and sits back on his haunches, slumps his shoulders, rests his palms on his thighs and whistles like a teakettle.

"I don't ask myself if it's perfect," he says. "I ask, 'Is it everything it could be?'"

He looks at his floor.

"This is as good as it gets."

SIX

DEREK OGDEN

TILTING AT WATERMILLS

Think of a clockmaker perched inside the works of a giant antique clock with gargantuan mechanical wheels and shafts, cogs and cants, gudgeons and gears, cranking and creaking and trembling. Derek Ogden is just now climbing inside such a machine, a watermill built in 1782 for grinding corn and wheat into meal and flour. At first glance, you wouldn't think of the Burwell-Morgan Mill as a machine. You'd think of it as a quaint limestone and clapboard building that stands along the banks of Spout Run in Millwood, Virginia, a burg of a few houses and a general store in the Shenandoah Valley, 50 miles west of Washington, D.C.

"People always regard a mill as another building," says Derek, a thin, taut man in worn pants and shirt, with wiry gray hair parted on the left and jutting out stiffly to the right. He clasps his bifocals tightly in his right hand. At 65, he is one of the world's preeminent millwrights. "A mill is not a building," he says. "A mill is a machine with a cover over it." With that, he scrambles across a railing and onto the framing of the new sluiceway he is building. In millwright parlance, it's known as the forebay or, as Derek prefers, the flume.

It's a 24-foot-long, four-ton canal of white oak, 42 inches wide and 24 inches high. When the mill is up and running, this flume carries three tons of water from the outside millrace to the top of the 20-foot-diameter wooden waterwheel. With the muscle of gravity and weight, the wheel turns and churns out 15 horsepower, which travels through a sequence of axles, monster wooden gears and spindles to turn two grinding stones that are adjusted to rotate one ten-thousandth of an inch above two stationary bed stones. The friction of the stones transforms grain into sustenance. Stone-grinding water mills based on the principles used at Burwell-Morgan date back 3,000 years.

"There must be easier ways to make a living," Derek says from his perch on the framing as he motions for the first of many 1 1/2-by-10-inch oak planks that will today become the floor of the new flume. "Let's see," he says, stroking his chin, pondering.

"You think she'll fit?" asks H. Baker, a retired army colonel who has volunteered to help. Derek flashes a wry smile and says, "Oh, yes, no doubt."

Derek Ogden first became fascinated with mills as a 15-year-old. He'd taken a trip from his home near Stratford-up-on-Avon in England to the Netherlands, where he saw the world famous windmills at Kinderdijk. "I wanted to know what made them tick," he says. After earning an engineering degree, he began to work with Rex Wailes, a legendary British millwright. Over the years, Derek repaired and restored scores of British mills, including the historic Chesterton Windmill at Warwickshire, built in 1632. He took a commission in Virginia to build the state's Flowerdew Post Windmill, commemorating the 1619 construction of the first English windmill built in North America. Derek and his wife never went back to England. They think of the States as home now. Besides, there are a lot of mills here that need work. In his adopted country, he has repaired dozens, including the Lee Mill at Robert E. Lee's estate in Stratford, Virginia, and George Washington's mill at Mount Vernon.

"Do you see the pencil?" he asks, searching around inside the flume. He's sitting on the first row of installed boards, his head and shoulders tucked down beneath the ceiling, a single workman's lamp illuminating his face. He has cut and lettered all the boards back in his shop near Madison, Virginia. He did his technical drawings and sketched the flume on a piece of notebook paper, which he keeps pulling out of his shirt pocket and consulting.

"All right," he says, folding and returning the sketch to his pocket. "Give me J."

Soon, an oak plank about 10 feet long and weighing perhaps 60 pounds is passed through the flume's framework. Like all the floor boards, it has been cut to length and planed to width. Its edges have been grooved to hold a 3/8-inch oak spline that will tongue the boards together tightly but also leave enough space between each so the floor can expand a total of half an inch along its four rows.

"What I really enjoy," Derek says of his work, "is that I can meet the original millwright. I never see him, but I know exactly what he was like by how he did his work." Derek believes he comes to know what kind of man that long-dead craftsman was by how closely he cut his mortises to his pencil markings, how expertly he used his chisels, how tightly he fashioned his joints. From such clues, he discerns the man's character, because a man's knowledge and dogged exactitude – his level of excellence – is how Derek judges character.

He has worked with helpers who will mark their cut lines on a board and then saw the board a good sixteenth of an inch off the mark. He simply cannot understand how the minds of such people work. It's no more difficult to saw on the line than to miss it. His attitude, by modern standards, is downright old world: "Any job done well, no matter how humble, is noble." Patience and the will to perfection equal achievement, which produces in people a joy that is loosely described as pride. So why not do it right?

In meeting the original millwrights, Derek has come across wooden joints so tight they haven't vibrated loose in 200 years. "They did it all by hand – the care they took, how accurate they were with a chisel." These are men he would like to know in person, men who could judge his work. Today, very few people know enough to judge his work. He is among the last of a species. In mills repaired by supposedly competent millwrights, Derek has seen joints so poorly made they've wobbled loose in a few years. He has seen new, tight gears made of green oak, which will inevitably shrink and loosen when the wood dries. He once knew a sawmill owner who could tell the tightness and strength of a tree's internal grain by studying the texture of its bark. "That's an art that's gone completely," he says sadly.

At the Burwell-Morgan Mill, Derek is denied the chance to meet the original builder. The mill was restored 30 years ago by well-meaning folks who saved the structure but little of the spirit of the original millwright's work. The machine has a long list of flaws. The flume Derek is replacing was rebuilt in pine instead of white oak. It leaked and rotted so badly it had to be lined with fiberglass. The spout that pours water from the flume into the buckets of the waterwheel delivers its load at 12 o'clock on the wheel rather than at the correct 11 o'clock position. The headgate that controls the flow into the flume from Spout Run is made of 20th-century metal instead of 18th-century oak. The wheel's oak axle, or shaft, is too small for the 20-foot wheel. The wheel itself is made of mahogany, a strong, water-resistant wood that was unavailable in 18th-century Virginia. The original wheel was surely white oak.

The waterwheel's spokes – its arms – are mortised and tenoned only a few inches into the wheel's shaft. They should extend all the way through in what's called a compass-arm fixing that interlocks in a notch joint, like the pieces of a three-dimensional wooden puzzle. In well-built mills, the moving millstones and gears aren't connected to the walls, floors or ceiling because the constant vibration will eventually cause the building to collapse, which is what happened to the Burwell-Morgan Mill in 1943. Today, the mill's moving parts are correctly attached to what's called the hurst frame, a giant stand-alone table to which the stones and gears are secured. But this hurst frame is far too tall, making it unstable. And those are just the big flaws. The good news is that the 2,000-pound, 100-year-old French buhrstones that mill the grain are in good shape, although their bearings need lubrication.

"People haven't paid enough attention to detail," Derek says of the mills he has repaired over the years. And they've got the wrong idea. They focus on saving mills instead of preserving and passing on the millwright's knowledge. But without the passing of skills, in 50 years no properly operating mill will be left in America.

From inside the flume, hammers begin clamoring, and their sound bounces painfully off bare wood and hard stone. Derek, H. Baker and two other local volunteers are all swinging away. They've laid three rows of planks and splines and must now pound wedges between the supporting frame and the third row of boards to raise the edge at about a five-degree angle. Only then is there room in the walled trough to tap the final row of grooved planks onto the protruding splines. Then they must knock out the supporting wedges so the interlocked floor can fall into place flush against both side walls, creating a watertight channel when the wood swells. Derek stops hammering, glances around in the flume, wipes sweat from his face and stretches his legs.

"I need a pencil—and a pair of younger knees."

When the flume is done, Derek will move on and repair the hurst frame for the next few months. Then he'll lug seven tons of oak planks and a giant three-foot-diameter oak log into the workshop in the woods behind his house and begin building Burwell-Morgan's new 20-foot waterwheel. He'll work alone for 12 or more hours a day, every day but Sunday. He'll use the dozens of gleaming tools that hang over the massive carpenter's bench he brought from England: the 100-year-old walnut-handled chisel that was his grandfather's, the engineer's square that his father bought in 1926. He'll move seemingly unmovable objects by himself on dollies or with a portable two-story crane. He'll stop occasionally and glance at the photograph of civil engineer Isambard Kingdom Brunel standing before the giant launching chains of the steamship *Great Eastern* in 1858. "He's my hero. The greatest engineer who ever lived, an absolute genius. He built tunnels, railroads, bridges, ships. He died at age 53 from overwork."

The Burwell-Morgan waterwheel will have 60 buckets configured as they were in 1782. The wheel's shaft will be 24 feet long, 28 inches across, made from a log that has been drying for two years. With two motors driving his six-foot chain saw, Derek will carve 12 sides into the log. Then he'll fine-sculpt it with two ancient millwrighting tools, a razor-sharp Kent broadax and an adze. All the pieces will be held together with wooden pegs or metal nuts and bolts that Derek will fashion in his metal shop. The waterwheel will be spoked with three 20-foot beams that pass through the center shaft in the compass-arm technique. To interlock them, Derek will saw and chisel a combination of 30- and 60-degree angle cuts in the arms – four cuts in the first, six in the next, six in the last. At the Burwell-Morgan Mill, he'll slide them all into a gaping hole sawed in the shaft's center, lock them together and then tightly wedge the gap closed.

"I get a great deal of satisfaction from it," Derek says. "When I put that joint together at the mill, I know it's going to be perfect."

And that, finally, is the kick. Derek once constructed a giant wooden swivel cap for the Danish Windmill in Elk Horn, Iowa. He built the whole contraption in his shop, re-machining the original 1824 cast-iron bearings upon which it would turn like a weather vane atop the 50-foot-high mill tower. He loaded it on a flatbed truck and shipped it out. As a crane lowered the cap into position, someone in the gawking crowd asked, "You think it will fit?"

"Of course it will fit," Derek answered.

"And it did, perfectly. I knew it would. I just looked at everybody else. Big smiles on everybody's faces and everybody shaking hands. It was like magic to them."

They were astounded, awed. Derek can think of only one comparison: Whenever he listens to Mozart's Clarinet Concerto K. 622, he feels an infinite sense of awe at its beauty. Always, chills run up his spine. "Brunel was the greatest engineer and Mozart was the greatest composer," he says. "I cannot believe that somebody could have written music as beautiful as that." When he finishes a project, Derek believes he feels a trace of what Mozart must have felt when he finished one of his works. How many people ever do anything that approaches perfection? How many ever feel that absolute joy? Derek wonders why anyone would want to live without experiencing it.

In two years, when he has finished the Burwell-Morgan Mill, Derek Ogden will again feel that joy. "They are all going to be standing there thinking, 'I wonder if it's gonna work?'

"And I know it will work."

The last row of the flume's floor is finally splined in place and held up in the air in its 5-degree tilt by the wedges beneath it. "Everybody off the flume," Derek says, as he climbs over its edge, hangs out over the 20-foot fall and, starting with the middle wedges to limit stress on the far ends of the splines, hammers them out as his helpers stand on the hurst frame and watch. The floor falls into place of its own weight like a ship being cast off from dry dock. When the headgate is eventually opened, the flume will leak water for about a week while the oak swells. Then it will stop leaking for about, oh, 25 years, when it will have to be replaced again if the history of the mill and the knowledge of the millwright are to stay alive.

"Perfect," Derek says of his day's work. "It's quitting time."

SEVEN

ROBERT READE

A CRAFTSMAN'S CONSCIENCE

The young men jump from the van and land with tool belts clanging, coveralls clean and ready for action, work boots stiff and shiny. Chattering enough that a cloud of fog rises from among them on a chilly Columbus, Ohio, morning, they deploy across a bed of golden straw to a stack of unfinished headers, a pile of waiting joists, and a beam of steel that spans the foundation of a house yet to be built. The men are quick to their work, quick to draw hammers and quick to make mistakes. Then comes Robert Reade, everything about him calm and deliberate. In his left hand dangles a tool belt as old as most of the nine men on his house-framing crew, a belt as thick and strong as a saddle girth and fretted from weather and wear. Amid the scurrying, he, at age 50, stands with his weight cocked on the right heel of boots that do not shine. He takes a final hit on his Camel, flicks it and, in one seamless motion, swings the belt and its tools around his rump, grabs the cincture in his right hand, ratchets the buckle pin into its eye and seats the whole clanking contraption with an imperceptible tug as he steps over a tire track cradling last night's rainwater. You'd have to be from Mars not to think of a cowboy packing six-guns.

"Let's do it," he says, his languid baritone laced with the musical drawl of a Virginia boyhood. "Let's knock this house out."

"Mr. Reade?" hollers Nathan Miller as he balances atop the steel foundation beam 10 feet above the basement floor. The name, as always, isn't said as a declaration but as a question.

"Mr. Reade?" yells Drew Poling.

"Mr. Reade?" cries Nick Gauder.

For the master framer, school is in session. Every work day for the last six years, Robert Reade has taught novice carpenters how to grasp a hammer, read a blueprint, snap a line, toenail a stud, sight the crown of a board. He leads one of 10 national programs aimed at upgrading the sorry state of house framing in the United States. The effort was launched after a Home Builders Institute study revealed that two of three builders felt forced to hire poorly skilled framers.

"When I frame a house, I feel a juice," Robert says, as he watches his crew lay out power saws and generators and 2 × 4s for the day's work. Before taking on the challenge of teaching young framers, Robert was building custom furniture and cabinetry. But he missed climbing acrobatically on the rafter-ribbing of a house. In his younger days, that always made him feel like an athlete, kept his senses sharp. The hammering made him feel not tired but robust. And calculating the roof rakes, square corners and rafter angles kept his brain humming.

"I can tell you something: There is nothing nicer-looking than a stick-built roof just sitting up there against the sky with no sheathing on it yet. It's a work of art. It's sad to cover it. When I see it, I feel what a potter must feel when he makes a pot, what a writer must feel when he writes a line. And now that I'm into the far half of my life, I want to pass that feeling on to these kids, to see their eyes turn bright." He laughs and runs an open hand through a full beard. "You know every time I finish a house, I stop and wonder to myself: Where does the space that new house occupies go? Is it lost, or has it moved someplace else? What happens to it?"

Then, once again, the reprise: "Mr. Reade?"

The steel beam that runs the width of the house doesn't fit into its foundation pocket, and Nathan says it's too long. Robert eyeballs it. "It's the angle, not the length." He grabs a circular saw and trims out a bite of the foundation's wooden sill board; the beam falls into place. All day, he is engaged in a kind of carpenter's Socratic dialogue.

Teacher: "How far is the fireplace cantilevered off the house?"

Student: "Two feet." Pause. "Ah, three feet?"

Teacher: "Let's go look at the plans." It's two feet.

Student: "I got to thinkin' too much."

Teacher: "Does this two-by-eight have a crown in it?"

Student: "I can't see it."

Teacher: "All right, everybody come look at this board."

Robert, a short, muscular man whose face is worn from the years of wind and rain and sun, lights a cigarette, tilts his head and blows smoke off into the pale blue sky. "Now this is where the craftsmanship comes in." And for 10 minutes he talks of boards and wood and trees. "A board is not a dead tree. It's like the caterpillar and the butterfly. It's at a different stage in its life." As he talks, one end of the 2×8 rests on the ground, edge up; the other end rests on his left shoulder, his left arm looped up and hooking the board's top edge at his wrist.

"See this grain," he says, stroking the gently sloping, elongated fibers with his fingertips. "It's talking to you." When it's tight and twirling, watch out. Saw that board and she'll cut loose like a taut spring, corkscrewing the wood. Always study the tip of a board. If the grain curves sharply, the board will likely cup – curve upward slightly at its edges – along its face against the direction of the tip's grain. When the grain on the face side rises uniformly, the board will likely crown – rise slightly – on its long edge with the grain's upward sweep.

But the rules of crowning and cupping differ with a board's use. Floor joists are always laid on their edges with the crown facing up, because they then make firmer contact with the flooring and resist sagging better. But 2×4s nailed face-to-face and used as vertical king and jack studs to support headers over windows and doors should always have their crowns facing opposite directions so they cancel each other out and create flat outside edges for nailing drywall and window trim. And the 2×6s or 2×8s that run flat atop the foundation should always lay with their crown edges facing into the house. That way, a sill board's crown never protrudes past the house perimeter to create a bulge in the wall.

"All right," Robert tells Nick, "look down the top edge of this board." Nick takes the board, holds one end to his eye and sights long-rifle-style down the edge toward the end resting on the ground. "See the crown?" Robert asks. Nick is upset. He can't see it. "Don't worry," Robert says. He takes his stringline and puts its end at the upper left-hand corner of the board's face. He has Nick hold it in place, then runs the line along the board's face to its opposite upper corner. When he does this, an infinitesimal rise in the board's edge appears above the string.

"Now look down that string. See the crown?"

"Yeah!" Nick shouts, all excited.

The men spread around the job – nailing and stacking window and door headers, sawing joists to length, laying out loose joists from center beam to outside walls, calculating the distance from the outside wall to the center of the fireplace, figuring the 45-degree-angle cuts for the corners of the bay window. Hammers are clattering, a portable generator is yammering, and the scent of fresh sawdust, an oddly sweet smell, hangs above the power saw. Robert and his men have already checked to see that the foundation is level. They've also determined that the foundation is about a half-inch shy of its planned width. To accommodate this, they have extended – floated is the framer's term of art – the sill plate boards, which must be flat and square, a quarter inch off each edge of the foundation. When the house is sided, the float won't be noticeable. It's only dangerous structurally if it extends more than an inch.

Although these beginning steps look simple, they are the most important in framing a house. "Everything after that just hangs on the frame," Robert says. But if the foundation isn't level, if the sill isn't square, if the joists aren't properly placed in relation to the plumbing, if the stud, door and window layouts aren't correctly pulled from the blueprints and marked on the sill, troubles rise to the roof. Robert stops to show a student how to ensure a straight power-saw cut by eyeing over the saw's blade, not its body. He stops to tell a student who has cut 11 feet of joist from a 16-foot board that he should have used a 12-footer, which would have left only one foot of waste. He stops to show two students carrying one 4×8 sheet of plywood how to hoist the sheet against the outside of a left shoulder, grasp the wood at the bottom with a left hand turned backward, and balance the board at the top with a right hand held across the chest. He stops to tell a student that he has cut a standard joist out of a piece of southern yellow pine that was supposed to support the bay window. "Don't be embarrassed," Robert says gently. "This is how we learn. But once you learn, don't ever do it wrong again. Even when nobody's looking."

Every man on every Robert Reade crew must come to understand all seemingly discrete details as pieces of a single frame. "If you can't visualize the completed project, how in the world can you build it?" He tells his crew: "When I build something, it's the second time I've seen it. The first time was up here." He touches his forehead. "It's not only the painter or the sculptor who has to visualize the finished object. It's the woodworker too. Yes, there is technique you need to know to use your tools." You must learn that a cat's paw won't crack wood if you run the paw with the grain, that a keel sheath with its thick crayon inside is needed to mark layouts distinctly, that a hammer must be gripped tight and loose at once, like a golf club, and that it should fall from the peak of its arc of its own weight, like a pendulum.

Knowledge matters.

"But there's also an attitude you need to do fine work," Robert says. "It's an artistic attitude." When a member of his crew can't envision how a double 2×6 header supports a window, Robert asks him to recall how the window trim looks inside a finished house, how the window looks in the wall, and then how the wall looks beneath the ceiling and above the floor. Robert trains his students to see the entire house and the place that one window header occupies, its niche. "How does it connect to everything else?" he asks.

Robert learned to think that way long ago. When he was 8, his dad – a navy officer, mathematician and amateur woodworker – built a small step stool for him so he could reach the controls of the table saw. "I can't remember not knowing how to run a table saw," he says. He and his dad built cabinets and chairs and a cedar chest Robert still keeps in his study. He once asked his father if he should fix a carpentry mistake he had made that was hidden from view. "You know it's there," his father said. Young Robert felt ashamed, and he fixed it.

At 14, he took a summer job doing scut work for a builder, who soon assigned him to work with an old carpenter, a Pennsylvania Dutchman named Orville Walters. The man taught him to change the blade of a power saw by propping the saw between his legs to keep both hands free. He taught him to pound a rectangular cut-nail into the foundation sill board with the nail's long face running with the grain so it wouldn't split the wood. He taught him a million tricks. And he told him: "Son, if you're gonna do this your whole life, swing a wooden-handled hammer. Nothing absorbs the shock to your arm like wood."

Robert went to Penn State, majored in economics and became an elementary school teacher. But he soon realized he enjoyed his summer carpentry work more. Over the next 25 years, he went from framing houses to building custom cabinets to making tables, desks and dressers. Then, in his framing teacher job, armed with a Hart 25-ounce framer – a hammer with a long, elegantly curved wooden handle – he rediscovered the rush of adrenaline that made him take up carpentry in the first place.

"It's addictive. You don't want to stop for lunch. It just feels so good. It comes from feelings of pride, but that's not all of it. It's emotional, almost spiritual. It's my connection to the cosmos." He laughs. "Maybe it comes from where that space goes that I'm taking up to build this house. Anyway, with this job, I can pass on that feeling, jump-start some people." Then, like a preacher calculating his conversions, he says, "Not all of 'em, but some of 'em."

Teacher: "How do you change decimals to fractions of an inch?"

Student: "You multiply by sixteen."

Teacher: "How long is the hypotenuse of the bay's forty-five-degree triangle?"

Student: "Ahhh…"

Teacher: "Square both sides, add them together and take the square root of that number to give you the length of the hypotenuse – thirty-three and fifteen-sixteenths, right?"

Student: "Ah, right."

By quitting time, the young men have something to show for their day's work. They've "rolled the joists" – laid them out face up from foundation to center beam and then, starting at one side of the house and stepping backward, one foot on the steel beam, another foot on the flat joist behind them, they have lifted and lapped the house's intersecting joists and nailed them in place. They've framed the fireplace and the bay window. Tomorrow, they'll lay the first-floor sheathing, gluing it to the joists and making sure to nail it down tight before the goop has had time to set. In the basement, they'll remove the nails that are bent like spider legs from the sill board down over the center beam. That way the nails won't squeak when people walk on the floor. They'll build the walls flat on the first floor, pulling the stud and door and window marks off the sill board. Then they'll raise them, square the corners with plywood sheets and march up the house, building stud on top of stud, rolling the joists on the second floor. Finally, they'll move into the roof rafters, with their angled cuts, compound joints and the constant danger of falling. "That's where you separate the men from the boys," Robert says. "Climbing around up there, it's got juice." The young men don't look juiced; they look scared.

"All right," Robert hollers, "let's get cleaned up."

The men scamper around, picking up trash and remnants of wood, putting away tools. They have the energy of puppies. More than anything, what the old dog wants to teach them – besides a million tricks – is shame. He wants them to feel ashamed when they miss a cut by an eighth of an inch, deface a stud with hammer scars or hide a shim under a joist. He wants to imbue them with a craftsman's conscience: Work well even when no one is looking.

Smoke in hand, Mr. Reade heads back to the van, steps over the tire track that has dried in the day's sun and unbuckles his tool belt, which falls around his rump as he lifts, swings, and lays the whole clanking contraption – with tape and stringline, cat's paw, keel and Hart hammer – open like a saddlebag over his left shoulder. "Every morning when I put on my tool belt," he says, "I tell myself that I am the best carpenter east of the Mississippi. Now, that's a cocky thing to say. But it pumps me up and sets the day's standard." He flicks his Camel, blows the last.

"That's what I want for these men."

EIGHT

LARRY STEARNS

MEDITATIONS IN COPPER

Smoke rises in signal puffs as Larry Stearns touches the bar of solder to the hot iron, turns the iron face down and watches the molten tin and lead flow like a glowing silver waterfall onto the copper beneath. There is a quick sizzle, and the sudden scent of hamburger cooking, as the paste flux burns away. The copper has already been heated to 414 degrees Fahrenheit with the iron, and the solder sweats into the seam like water climbing the roots of a tree. Larry brands the hot iron to the seam for an instant, just long enough to let a gray, pencil-thin line of liquid solder bleed along the seam's outer edge. He lays the solder bar on the workbench, returns the iron to its perch, takes off his leather gloves and examines the octagonal cone he is constructing for a three-foot-tall finial. When finished, it will grace the rooftop of a computer magnet's mansion on Long Island.

"Not bad," Larry says, running his fingers along the now hard, cool and perfect line of solder. "No one will see that seam when it's 30 feet off the ground, but I'll know it was done right."

Larry Stearns is a coppersmith. The word sounds quaint today, imported from a past of Victorian row houses and Queen Anne mansions whose peaks and spires often boasted decorative finials or weather vanes. But for years, from his shop on Machia Hill in the Vermont forest outside Burlington, Larry has made a modern living at an antique craft.

His 16-foot-high weather vane sits atop Boston's Arlington Street Church; for Chicago's St. Ignatius Preparatory School he made a 14-foot-high repoussé finial; and the city hall in Lancaster, Pennsylvania, carries his Tower Belvedere, a replica of a leafed, copper-clad dome that took 4,000 pounds of copper and 500 pounds of solder to build. These aren't mass-produced hardware-store ornaments; these are sculptures – metal creations cut and bent by hand and pounded into their designs by hammers of 50 sizes and shapes.

"I love copper," Larry says. "To take a flat sheet and bring it to life, to see it transformed, is terribly gratifying." Larry, now 40 years old, smiles, knowing that he, too, has been transformed by the strong, lustrous, malleable and corrosion-resistant metal that man has molded into weapons, tools and decorative objects for 6,000 years.

"I used to be a party-loving roofer," he says. "I did a quality job, but I never thought about doing anything in terms of more than how much money I was going to make. I had pride in my work, but it was an egotistical pride – I can do this! It was not the right attitude." He pauses to ponder exactly what he means. "I lacked humility. Ultimately, that leads to an attitude of 'That's good enough,' an attitude that says people don't know the difference between good and bad quality – if they like it, I like it. For me, the change came when I realized that what I do in this life is important to nobody else but me. I don't sign my work unless I'm asked. It's not the person, it's the work that should last. That's the humility I had to learn."

As he works on the finial this morning, in a shop filled with hand-operated machines that crease and cut, roll and spin copper, Larry is surrounded by weather-vane patterns as traditional as a trotting horse and as whimsical as an Egyptian warrior. Giant sheets of salmon pink copper, with reflective surfaces that make tall, thin men look short and squat, go boi-yoi-yoiing as they are moved from storage to workbench. His two assistants hammer dissonantly on other projects. But Larry is oblivious to the distractions and focuses on the finial.

Using the ancient Pythagorean theorem, he has already transferred a two-dimensional rendition of the finial into a three-dimensional pattern. He has cut a fan-shaped, .0216-inch-thick sheet of copper to match the pattern, bent it from bottom to peak along eight 40-degree hip lines and spot-soldered the resulting octagonal cone at a point halfway between the top and bottom of the overlapping hip run. This copper cone, 23 3/8 inches across at its base and rising 19 1/2 inches to its peak, will be the finial's bottom. An 8-inch-diameter cylinder will cover its peak and rise like a stovepipe 14 inches, although only 7 1/2 inches will be visible, with the rest giving structural support. Half-round ornaments will encircle the cylinder at its base and at the top of its exposed rise. Above the upper half-round will rest an octagonal, outward-sweeping soffit that will rise 2 7/8 inches. Atop the soffit will rest an 8-inch-high octagonal cone. At its truncated peak, appearing to balance delicately, will be a 3-inch-diameter ball.

In the way that an engineer's sketch can't evoke the final towering majesty of a church steeple, mathematics can't evoke the eventual beauty of Stearns's finial. It will glint in the sunlight like a bright new penny until the rain calls from within it a vague and then deep green patina that will take 20 years to mature. The finial will be strong enough to withstand winds and storms for more than 100 years, outliving its creator.

"When I'm doing this it's meditative," Larry says, as he puts his gloves back on, takes up the hot iron and the solder bar and poises like a surgeon over the open end of the large octagonal cone. "The repetitiveness is calming. The further you get into it, the more addictive it is."

The single spot of solder he has pressed at the center of his cone's closing hip run is melted smooth. He has tacked the cone there because the iron's heat must be distributed equally along the hip's length otherwise heat expansion will cause the copper to buckle. Now, smoke rising and flux sizzling, he tacks the seam at its peak and base, continuing to split the difference between tacks until he has created a single, gleaming line.

"It looks good," he says.

This finial, with its mostly flat surfaces, will take him a day's labor – eight hours. To build the 16 large, three-dimensional leaf pods that surround the base of Lancaster City Hall's dome, Larry hammered for more than 500 hours. The edges of the leaves had to curve naturally, and the veins that run along each leaf lobe had to look delicate and alive. He shaped them by hammering copper into "negative forms" – the concave sides of bowl-shaped wooden casts of all sizes. He used oval-shaped hammers, hammers with pointed tips, hammers with chisel tips, hammers with slight curves and hammers with large curves. In the way that a cloth napkin would have to be pleated and folded with fingers to fit inside a salad bowl, the copper had to be pleated and then smoothed with hammer strokes.

People think of copper as a solid material, but it's malleable. Although hammering work-hardens copper and makes it brittle, heating the metal to at least 392 degrees and cooling it – annealing it – softens the copper for further sculpting. The base of Larry's St. Ignatius repoussé finial in Chicago, for instance, has copper ribs that curve both horizontally and vertically. During hundreds of hours of hammering, each rib had to be annealed four times before Larry could fashion the proper compound curves. "I read somewhere that Michelangelo said he stayed fit mentally and physically because of the hammer," he says. "I can understand that now. Hammering is good for the soul. I go into another place – hammer and anneal, hammer and anneal. I get possessed. I can go on for hours."

Larry didn't always take his work so seriously. An A-student in high school, he went to college, dropped out and began working as an itinerant roofer. While installing a copper roof on a Long Island mansion, he met a Czechoslovakian sculptor who was creating statues for the estate and a second man who was the project's contractor. In his spare time, Larry went to Manhattan art galleries with the sculptor, who derided the pop art they often saw. In one gallery an artist displayed a leather couch surrounded by a red movie theater rope.

"Trash!" the sculptor declared.

In his view, the artist couldn't have made an emotional connection to that piece of junk; connecting emotionally to one's work was the sculptor's definition of art, whether you were painting pictures, carving stone or installing a copper roof. At the same time, the contractor for whom Stearns worked kept telling him work wasn't only a way to make a living but a path to life's meaning. Put yourself into what you create, he said, because your creations aren't only objects; they are archeological evidence of your humanity. You can go through life lazy and kicking and screaming, he told Larry, or you can go through life with passion for what you do. Larry could feel something stirring.

"Before, I always felt like I was doing a job. I didn't like it. I wanted to turn over a rock and find a pile of gold and retire to a Caribbean island." Then one day, imbued with his mentors' preaching, he was atop the mansion's roof trying to figure out how – without cutting, splicing and caulking the roof's copper sheeting – he could sculpt the metal with his hammer up the rise, across the run and around the corner of about 50 steps that were part of the masonry chimney. He had no idea. Then, on the roof that day, he simply knew the answer. He began to hammer and smooth the copper in a way that allowed it to turn and curve without wrinkling, to flow into itself like water. He hammered and smoothed, losing track of time. It remains the second most thrilling moment of his life, ranking behind only the birth of his son.

"It's hard to put into words. I had this emotional feeling in my chest. I knew that this was a revelation of some kind. I didn't know what, but I did know that if I hadn't begun to care about what I was doing, I would never have discovered it. It was so incredible. It was the turning point in my career. And I was doing it because of this new attitude." He knows it sounds wifty, but it was as if the work spoke to him, decided to reveal its answer. Larry felt humbled, awed and exhilarated. "It's in here," he says, touching his chest. "It's like a drug, an emotional high."

When Larry returned to Vermont a decade ago, he was still installing roofs, but he was also building his shop on Machia Hill. Today, keeping up with orders for his signature line of weather vanes and finials, which begin at $380, as well as creating far more expensive custom pieces and doing historic restoration work, keeps him and three workers busy year-round. Epiphanies like the one on the Long Island roof are rare. But sometimes, such as the other night as he worked alone on a mock-up of a custom whirligig, he feels a trace of the original passion, the emotional connection to his work that changed his life forever. That night in the shop, he lost track of time, looked up and saw that four hours had passed. He felt refreshed.

"At those moments, I feel like an artist," he says.

Larry has stacked the now finished octagonal cones, cylinder, half-round ornaments and the soffit on the workbench in their final order. He stands back, studies his work and decides that it is good. "I don't think it matters what you do," he says. "Some doctors are artists, some are just walking through. People who are motivated work with all their hearts.

"On the journey of life, that's the definition of an artist."

NINE

JEFF GAMMELIN

A FIREPLACE STANDS 2,000 YEARS

A mountain is rising in the living room. Waist-high boulders have been laid as jambs on either side of a yawning fireplace mouth. Overhead, through a hole in the high roof, a gargantuan beam of Maine's Deer Isle granite as long as a sofa and as heavy as a car hangs motionless on the end of a descending cable. That stone – 9 feet, 2 inches long; 20 inches high; 10 inches thick; 2,228 pounds – will span the jambs as the lintel of this monumental fireplace. Around those stones, 47 huge rocks will be laid 10 feet high and 11 feet wide, creating the illusion that you are at the entrance to a cave, that you are standing before the rocks of Stonehenge, that you are staring up at the giant, broken steps of Chichen Itza. A year from now, when the house is done, a fire blazes and people sit comfortably with the lights dimmed and gentle music playing, they will at times be transported, feel as if they are not outside that cave looking in but inside that cave, surrounded by stone, safe.

"I don't think it's gonna torque," Tom Brennan says in the here and now. He cranes his neck to study the suspended lintel. Behind the stone, through the hole in the mansion's otherwise finished roof, clouds in the gunmetal seacoast sky scud past.

"We'll see," Jeff Gammelin, the monument's creator, says softly.

He stands a few steps back from Tom, looking up and then panning down across the exposed first-floor ceiling beams that run perpendicular to the fireplace's still naked cinder-block tower. The lintel slab must be snaked down through those beams along the side of the blocks, swiveled 90 degrees and then brought to rest on the jambs.

"Swing to the right!" Tom yells to the boom jockey. "Hold it!"

The crane goes mute, the lintel stone tugs and halts, and the cable ripples along its length like a flexing muscle. Even in the silence, Jeff's voice is almost inaudible.

"We're there."

He takes off his right glove, reaches out and touches the lintel stone with his fingertips. It's cold, the surface sharp with deep-green lichen that has colonized the rock for who knows how many eons. It grows like a miniature forest atop the erratic ravines and rises of the stone's face, which has not been cut by diamond blade or spalled by rosebud torch, scored by carbide trace or fractured by feather and wedge. It is natural rock, a ledge, an outcropping, a seismic fissure – fireplace as ornamental geology.

Jeff Gammelin is a small and wiry 47-year-old who today wears tan work pants, a black sweatshirt, Nikes and a San Francisco baseball cap cocked back on his head. After decades of hefting and lugging stones for the hundreds of fireplaces his Freshwater Stone & Brickwork has built in homes around Orland, Maine, his muscles are large on his small frame. Over the years, Jeff has gone from building fireplaces with stones that one man can carry to building fireplaces with stones that only boom trucks can lift. He has gone from using stones shaped by nature to boulders he and his men sculpt with fire and tools. He has built with bigger and bigger stones not only because it is his vision but also because new equipment and tools have made it possible. Yet that mastery and growth of craft doesn't explain what drives him never to build again what he has built before, doesn't explain his obsession with never settling.

"I don't understand it myself," he says. "It's grow or die."

He removes his hand from the lintel, puts on his glove. "A good stone," he whispers.

"Boom up!" Tom now hollers. "We gotta scoot it the width of a line." Tom, a master stonemason who has been with Jeff for 11 years, leans close to the lintel, squinting to check the layout marks that signal its proper location on the jambs. Nothing on this fireplace – whose chaotic stonework makes it the most unusual Jeff has ever designed – or any of his fireplaces is left to chance. Each stone has been marked for its exact left-to-right, front-to-back position. Each rock's precise depth, angle and cant has been determined back in the shop. The fireplace was mocked up, the stones numbered and diagrammed, then dismantled and shipped to the house, where this week it will be reconstructed to within a sixteenth of an inch of the original layout.

Jeff began making mock-ups eight years ago when a skeptical architect had trouble visualizing what a certain design would look like. Jeff laid out the fireplace on the ground and raised the architect on a forklift. After that, he mocked up all his fireplaces in the shop. No more hauling tons of stone to jobsites, angering contractors for taking up too much space. No more spur-of-the-moment decisions.

"We gotta go a quarter inch," Tom yells. He squints and cranes his head again, hollers, "Take it up!"

Sometimes, in quiet moments late at night or on long drives on winding rural roads, Jeff thinks about what he has accomplished since he and his wife, Candy, packed up their old Datsun after college and wandered the East Coast looking to buy land in the country. Prices didn't get low enough until Maine, where their quest ended in a wooded, rocky pasture – 80 acres for $16,000. No sewer, water, electric or gas. They got jobs as teachers. Jeff built a windmill for power, had a well drilled and built the two rooms they called a house. In the winter, they'd awaken with snow on their blankets.

A few years later, he decided to use the stones littering his land to build a fireplace, around which he planned to erect a real house. He had grown up in a New Jersey lake-retreat-turned-suburb, where the original bungalows and their fireplaces had been made with rugged native stone and rustic timbers. With this image in mind, he began to build. No wimp of a fireplace, either, but a muscular 16-foot-tall, 12-foot-wide fireplace. He walked his land, stone-picking – fat stones, flat stones, long, short, round, jagged stones, white, gray, brown, a vein of lavender, a swath of pink. He built his fireplace with a mind as clear as water – no experience, no knowledge, no preferences in texture, color or shape, no claims to art.

Then one day, standing in the second story of a barn he'd built, Jeff looked across the field at his nearly finished fireplace, which stood like a reverse ruin, rising, not falling. Suddenly, he saw consciousness at work. The rocks had runs that traveled like grain in a crosscut of wood, chaotic yet orderly. Large stones coursed heavily and then blended into rivers of gentler, smaller stones that gave way to stones of still more shapes and sizes, all of them woven together by streams of mortar that Jeff had blindly troweled stone to stone. From the distance, the rocks of many colors lost their craggy personalities and became a single canvas resembling the bold, natural colors of a Gauguin painting. Stunned, he thought, *Maybe I could do something with this.*

He built a fireplace for a friend. Then he got a paying customer. He quit teaching. In the decades since, he has never been without work. From building a fireplace in his own house with scavenged stones, he went on to build $70,000 fireplaces in vacation homes of the painlessly wealthy. More important, he went from building with unselfconscious intuition to working with a conscious philosophy, with one hard-fast rule: Each fireplace must be different, in either grand or trivial ways, from the last.

"You're there!" Tom hollers as the massive descending lintel comes to rest on the jambs.

"No," says Jeff, "we're in too far."

He grabs a crowbar, wedges it between lintel and jamb and begins to "walk" the lintel away from the cinder-block tower. Tom, the fussbudget of the two, is cringing, afraid Jeff will chip the rock's face. This fireplace may be Jeff's creation, but it's Tom's baby. Jeff doesn't build his fireplaces alone, nor does he envision them alone. The couple who own this house, for instance, wanted a unique fireplace. Jeff did several designs using long, narrow stones to mimic the house's ceiling beams. No go. The wife decided she wanted the new fireplace to remind her of the one Jeff had already built in their nearby studio house. It was a huge, flat-faced, rustic but formal fireplace made of a dozen giant, dark granite "tailings" – stones cut and left as waste in an old quarry operation. She also wanted the fireplace-in-progress on the first floor linked to the upstairs fireplace, which was designed by the architect to be built at a 45-degree angle to the fireplace beneath it.

Jeff's solution: At the jambs, the lintel and the upper left of the fireplace, he used granite boulders like those in the formal studio fireplace. But at the upper inside corner of the right jamb is a slightly cantilevered stone that looks as if it has broken off and is about to slide onto the hearth. The lintel is actually resting on the right jamb, but the one-ton rock looks as if it's sitting tenuously on this splinter of stone, which is secured to the jamb with a stainless-steel pin. That's the first hint that something strange is going on. Above the lintel, the dark, staid stones on the left transform in the center into smaller, rugged, more colorful stone fingers that, like a volcanic eruption, suddenly shoot up from horizontal to vertical and tip, twist and cantilever every which way, as if they're about to tumble to the floor. Like a book, the fireplace reads from left to right – from predictability to chaos, conformity to nonconformity. Moving to the far right, the stones eventually extend two feet beyond the front plane of the fireplace and turn to a 45-degree angle, creating the illusion that they support the fireplace upstairs.

Tom asked Jeff, "Where'd you get the idea?"

"I closed my eyes and got it."

The men spent a week in the shop moving stones in and out, as if they were trying on different costumes. Tom gathered the stones and Jeff selected from among them, decided their horizontal or vertical angle, their forward tilt. Then Tom used an oxy-propane torch to fit each stone against those next to it. The heat dries out moisture near the surface of the rock and causes it to flake off in fine layers, which leaves a natural-looking edge. He used a German set chisel, a hammer and arm muscle to break away large chunks of stone. To make clean cuts, he used a carbide trace and a hammer to score a fine line and then pounded V-shaped feather and wedge anchors into holes drilled along that line, fracturing the stone crisply. He cut the jambs on their outer sides to fit them to length and rubbed the edges with shards of granite to hide the fresh cuts. It is a Jeff rule: No stone face and no run of jamb or lintel that faces the firebox is ever touched.

"They'll stay green with lichens forever," he says.

When Jeff began stonework, he wasn't such a perfection-ist. His father had owned an appliance store, and the son was always amazed at the intensity with which the man worked. But Jeff eventually discovered the same intensity in himself. He studied Gauguin's paintings and saw in "Jacob and the Angel," "Siesta, Tahiti" and "Riders on the Beach" the colors and shapes he wanted to see in his fireplaces. He studied photos of stone walls in Ireland and England, the monoliths of Stonehenge. He scoured the Maine countryside for stone houses and walls to see how they'd been built. He examined the geometry of moun-tainsides, how renegade rocks jut and flare. He wandered rocky blueberry bogs and found stones split like onions by weather and time into layers – stones that could be reconstructed, as if to thwart geological time.

He decided he hated stonework that "floated" in thick veins of mortar, because the stones didn't touch, didn't look as if they were standing of their own weight, one atop the other, as God would lay them. He decided that stonework is a chan-nel to something primal in people. His customers talked of the comfort they felt sitting before his fireplaces, as if they were in-side a cave with a fire burning, or walking along a rocky shore-line from childhood, or stumbling upon a basseting outcrop of stone while hiking in the woods.

For years, Jeff felt it was a privilege just to have the chance to build a fireplace. He got more practical with age and three daughters. He better calculated costs and profits and health plans. But he wonders if he ever would have gotten to where he is today – with 22 employees and a $1.5-million-a-year business

– if it had not been for his obsession with never building this time what he had built last time.

"I doubt it," he says. Jeff gives people what they want; it's their home. "But the challenge is not to sit on what you've done. You have to control your materials, tools, vision and situation. You have to grow on the craft end to do more on the creative end." Investing in cranes, for instance, has allowed him to build with stones as heavy as 10 tons, giving him more creative freedom. Diamond-blade saws cut thick granite stones that steel blades never could. Modern torches allow more subtle shaping of stones than chisels. "But tools are tools. They're meant to take you where you want to go. What comes first is the drive to keep yourself interested, to still be a little sad when the workday ends, to never lose touch with the thrill of doing it."

This fireplace has been a thrill to build. The boom cable is gone, and Jeff and Tom have troweled mortar between the jambs and the now-seated lintel. They've pargeted mud on the cinder blocks behind the rocks and filled the several-inch cavity between tower and stone. They're now on their knees pointing the mortar between the stones inside the fireplace's mouth. Tom uses a mason's tuck trowel. Jeff uses the handle of a soup spoon, his tool of preference since he built his own fireplace decades ago.

"I still hate floaters," he says. He wants each stone to sit on the stone below in at least two places. His trademark technique for making the structure look as if it's resting upon itself is to scrape the mortar in the joints back to where the stones come closest to touching. He wants only a tissue-thin layer of mortar between the rocks at their points of contact so the human eye has the impression that they are piled naturally. Then it doesn't matter how wide or narrow are the rest of the mortar joints, because the fireplace will always look as if it's standing of its own weight. Finally, finished for the day, the two men step back to admire their work.

"Oh," says Tom, "it looks so nice."

Jeff nods, a little sad the day's work is done.

TEN

LORNA KOLLMEYER

CASTING FOR BEAUTY LOST

She talks to herself while she works. Mumbles, really, through the long, elegant fingers of her right hand held to her mouth, her left forearm spanning the waist of her lean 6-foot, 1-inch frame, an athlete's frame. "OK, who goes where?" she asks, reaching out, plucking up and relocating a piece of the twirling-floral Victorian frieze that is spread like a three-dimensional puzzle on the worktable. "This little guy goes here. And this fellow goes next to him." She straightens up, closes an eye. "Let's move this little sucker." She gently twists the corner of an acanthus stem where it kisses a nasturtium bud. Then, reaching across her body with her right arm, she jacks up the left leg of her jeans, hoists her work-boot-shod foot onto the table, rests her left elbow on her bent knee and stares.

"So how does this damned thing go together?" She stands down on both feet, arms akimbo. "There's something gratifying in getting that acanthus stem to turn just right. Your mind is a little muddy, you can't see the solution and then suddenly it's clear."

Poof!

"That's the feeling I love."

Lorna Kollmeyer, one of the nation's finest ornamental plaster artisans, is the modern embodiment of Italy's 15th-century *stuccotori*, who resurrected the plaster-molding techniques of ancient Greece and Rome, allowing for the creation of mammoth columns and statues, as well as delicate wall and ceiling reliefs, at a fraction of the cost of traditional stone carving. This particular morning, Lorna has been in her shop moving pieces, mumbling to herself for four hours. She is almost satisfied with the layout of the intricate 10 × 24-inch pattern she'll soon reproduce in plaster to run above the picture rail high on the dining room walls of the elegant Shannon-Kavanaugh House on San Francisco's famous Postcard Row.

The frieze pattern, supplied by the owner of the house, was jumbled in shipping. After Lorna pieces it back together, she must cast the pattern in 2-foot sections of plaster that can repeat seamlessly along the wall as if the frieze's swirling tendrils, leaves and flowers had no beginning or end. She must outline the frieze on its backing board and heat, soften and press the pieces back into place. Only then can she brush liquid urethane onto the pattern to create a mask that will be pulled away and then used like a JELL-O mold to cast plaster images.

"Maybe I can cheat this down," Lorna says to herself.

"That appears to fit," she answers.

"Maybe I can split the difference."

"That's lookin' pretty good."

"Go down a little, come up."

She shrugs, smiles. "I mumble to myself."

Two decades ago, the 39-year-old craftswoman was an all-American basketball player at Colorado College with a jump shot smooth and silky. And she was a Phi Beta Kappa who wrote her undergraduate thesis on how William Wordsworth and Charles Dickens portrayed England's transformation from agrarian to industrial society. She was always going to do something BIG with her life. Her dad was a Los Angeles pipe fitter, a blue-collar guy who worked with his hands and expected the young and gifted Lorna to make the great American leap: He wanted her to work with her brains not her muscles, her head not her hands.

Lorna never made that leap. After college, she played pro basketball in France for a year and planned to get a college coaching job. But basketball had been the focus of her life since she was 11, and she wanted to try something new. So she landed in San Francisco, where she had friends, and took a job on a house remodeling crew. Never a prissy-pot, Lorna hammered nails, sawed trim, refinished floors, cold-tarred roofs and sheetrocked walls. "I really loved it," she says. "Being fit and hammering nails and understanding how something went together."

Then 14 years ago, without realizing she was making a choice that would change her life, Lorna bought a friend's fledgling ornamental plaster business for $1,000, and he spent two days teaching her how to mold brackets and ceiling medallions. Soon after, on a whim, she bid on a job to restore the plaster "bits and bobs" of San Francisco's historic Hotel Majestic. Surprise – her $22,000 bid won. She panicked. The next lowest bid had been $56,000. And she had no experience making the scores of Victorian ornaments she'd promised – medallions, rosettes, cartouches, finials, moldings, plaques, capitals, scrolls, spandrels and corbels.

Lorna marshaled the same laser-sharp concentration, attention to tiny details and ability to work long unbroken hours that had made her a precision athlete. Overnight, she created a factory, rented a shop in a former Navy shipyard in San Francisco and called on an army of friends. Working from old photographs, two friends who were artists and sculptors carved reliefs of mermaids and scrolls and baskets of fruit from clay. Lorna learned to sculpt acanthus leaves and scrollwork herself, discovering that she had a natural artistic touch and an eye for proportion. Then she made molds and casts. Her contract called for all objects to be soaked in boiled linseed oil and, taking the charge literally, she dipped each piece in a kiddie pool of oil. Only later did she realize she was expected only to brush on the weatherproofing liquid.

"To this day, I can't stand the smell of linseed oil," she says, laughing. Lorna still finds it nearly impossible to believe that she got the job done, laboring night and day for five months. "The universe smiled my way," she says. "The Majestic put me on the map."

This morning, back in her shop, Lorna jury-rigs a stove to heat and soften her frieze for application to its wood backing. She takes a 5-gallon plastic bucket, puts a spouting teakettle inside, stretches nylon mesh over the bucket's mouth and lays out pieces of frieze like so many strips of bacon on a grill. When the pieces are hot and juicy, she scrapes them off the screen with a 6-inch drywall blade cum spatula, lays them back inside their penciled outlines and gently presses them into place, careful not to leave prints. As she steams, scrapes and presses, as the goop rides up and hardens under her fingernails, she talks.

"After the Majestic, I got better at plaster."

She mastered the techniques of mold making, learned to alternate thin and thick coats of latex or polyurethane to make the mold strong enough to remove without tearing. She learned to remove old paint by pouring boiling water over an object. She discovered that she had an artist's eye for re-sculpting the flowers and vines, faces and bodies of old and damaged ornaments.

"But I was still tortured," she says.

Although she was making as much as $60 an hour, success seemed to her a leather briefcase, clicking heels on marble hallway floors, fashionable clothes and a wide-windowed office. She touches the blue collar of her work shirt and laughs. Her pipe-fitter dad would just shake his head, baffled. "We spent $25,000 on college so she could be a plasterer," he'd say. "I could have taught her to be a plasterer."

Lorna decided: "What I'm doing isn't really good enough." So she got a friend to run the business, moved to London and studied computer animation. As time went on, she began to see her electronic images as lifeless. She couldn't touch them, hold them in her palms, run her fingertips over their nooks, feel roughness where she had failed, smoothness where she had succeeded. In San Francisco, she had been surrounded by her plaster sculptures – gargoyles high on rooftops, garlands and berries, roses and lamb's tongue, a fairy riding a dolphin, a mermaid, a seahorse, pineapples and seashells, a wild pig, wreaths and laurels, a man playing a lute, cherubs, angels, an elephant and an owl, Madonna, Venus, Apollo and Buddha.

"My work was more of my identity than I gave it credit for," she says, as she deftly works teardrop buttons of modeling clay into tiny fractures in her frieze, simultaneously pressing and smoothing the clay with "toolie" – a spatula the size of a small fingernail file. "My work was a lot more gratifying than what I was seeing in the great world of computer animation, which I had thought was so glamorous. There was a whole epiphany about me struggling all day to make something on the computer, and it just didn't mean anything to me. I got over being embarrassed about working with my hands. I decided to take great pride in it."

She flew home from London with a new attitude: *I'm not making plaster doodads for a living; I'm resurrecting 19*[th] *century Victorian history.* Lorna now has more than 50 original San Francisco ceiling medallions, each named after the street it originally came from – Broderick, Page, Hayes, Laguna, Anza, Hartford, Scott, Water, Ellis and Steiner, medallions that come in intertwining leaves and garlands, grapes and pears, lilies, roses, palms, cattails, daisies, acorns, seashells, storks and an endless array of geometric designs. She also has collected and reproduced 75 original corbels and hundreds of other ornaments.

"I want a collection of real San Francisco patterns. The beautiful things in this city just about bring tears to my eyes. There were people all over the city, mostly European immigrants, creating these ornaments, coming up with ideas and designs that were unique to San Francisco. We know nothing about these people today, but we have their work. It's a legacy for me.

"That is the quest."

Right now, Lorna seems like the last candidate for a hero's journey. Having donned a black pig-snout respirator, a plaster-caked apron and rubber gloves, she begins to brush urethane over the frieze – a thin layer to coat the intricate details, then heavier coats that don't drip even when she turns her brush over and back. Her voice gurgles up as if from deep water.

"So much of this is just plain hard work." She'll get an old piece and spend days laboriously removing 120 years of paint, layer after layer. Then she'll patch the cracks and holes – and sometimes the piece will be more cracks and holes than not. "What's gratifying, after all the back-breaking labor, is making it look perfect again."

Poof!

"The joy is seeing this lovely thing."

Outside her shop an hour later, in San Francisco's summer sunshine, Lorna breathes the fresh air deeply. She can smell the brackish bay and the sourdough bread cooking at the Parisian Bakery. "I like answering to my own standard. I once worked in a bike shop, and even when there wasn't any work to do, when the shop was in order and there were no customers, I wasn't allowed to read a book. I had to pretend I was organizing the shorts. It was demeaning. I used to stand in that shop and time just went tick, tick, tick for hours. So boring. Now I blink my eyes at 3 o'clock and I think, *Where did the day go?* The lure of working at some bureaucratic job or in a bank is not for everybody. I would have withered and died on the vine at a 9-to-5 job where I had to show up at exactly the same time and have a 15-minute coffee break between 10 and 10:15 and a half-hour lunch between 12 and 12:30. It would have crushed my spirit."

Tomorrow morning, the mold Lorna made from the frieze will be cast in plaster. It will harden and the rubbery mask will be peeled off, revealing the twirling-floral Victorian adornment that will rim the dining room walls of the elegant house on Postcard Row.

Poof!

And Lorna will mumble to herself, "I made this."

ELEVEN

PETER GOOD

HE BUILDS
BEAUTIFUL DOORS

"W hat makes you think I'm eccentric?"

Peter Good asks this question as he removes his glasses and, with rotating thumbs, polishes away a fine film of sawdust. He returns the glasses to his face and smiles. Leaning against his shoulder is one of two Honduran mahogany doors he made for fun more than a decade ago. He built and shipped the doors to Brazil, where the esteemed sculptor Paulino Lazur carved elaborate designs into them – months of work that cost Peter $3,600. The doors came back as beautiful as he had imagined. Ever since, he has been shuttling them out of the way in his cramped workshop in Oakland, California. They're still for sale at $12,600 each, although he might let them go for less.

"You want eccentric?" he asks. "I'll show you eccentric."

In 23 sawdust-caked boxes in Peter's sawdust-caked workshop are 11,000 electron tubes that he plans to incorporate into several doors. For one door, he plans to station about 100 tiny tubes in parallel rows between two pieces of glass held together by a wooden frame, then pour clear liquid plastic resin between the glass. The resin will harden, encasing the tubes in a transparent tomb.

"Won't that make a neat door?"

Then there's the door diagram that he drew after seeing *Star Wars*. He liked the scene in which Han Solo and Chewbacca are escaping from the Death Star and outrun the Storm Troopers as a door behind them appears to close in a diamond shape from four directions. That door fascinated Peter, who figured out that it was most likely an optical illusion created by panels that opened and shut sideways on a rolling track. He was going to build a model to recreate the illusion and send a video to *Star Wars* creator George Lucas, but he never got around to it.

"I wanted to say, 'Hi, George. I figured out your doors!'"

And, finally, there's the door that began as one thing and is becoming something else entirely. Peter planned to build a door with a stained glass scene of a stream running from a mountain waterfall through a jungle into a series of bubbling pools. Then he got to thinking: Wouldn't it be interesting if real water were running in the stream inside the door? And wouldn't it be even more interesting if the stream's water actually ran outside the glass? Physics commands that water adhere to virtually any surface. But what about the splash when the door opens and closes? Well, why not have an electric eye that turns off the water pump when people get within, say, 10 feet and doesn't turn the pump back on until the door closes behind them. *Hey, I can do that*, Peter thought. And so he is, although he has no idea who will buy it. He again rotates his thumbs to clean his glasses and smiles.

"See, I'm not eccentric."

Peter Good builds beautiful doors. "Doors are the only thing I do." For 28 years, he has built 10 to 30 custom doors a year. Most are straight-ahead doors for people's houses – doors of fir, pine, walnut, mahogany, rosewood and teak, but doors that can't be bought in stores, doors that boast a creator's touch. Each costs $3,000 to $15,000. Peter works 7 a.m. to 4 p.m. weekdays, no weekends. He takes three vacations a year to New York, one to Hawaii. But he has no sick leave, no paid vacation, no company retirement. He pays for his own insurance. He is not rich, but he has never thought about working to become rich. "I thought about doing what I wanted to do. It's a matter of where your values lie." At 59, Peter believes his life is nearly perfect. "I am a fortunate man."

He works alone in his shop, a small, white, peeling garage that from the outside looks as if it might fall over. Inside, it looks as if it might be held together by spider webs and sawdust. Except for his cat Minou, Peter doesn't want visitors. And for a practical reason: He can't talk and do much else at the same time. When he talks and drives, for instance, he always ends up going slower and *sloower* and *slooower*, until his wife finally says, "Peter, speed up." So he sure can't talk and run a table saw. Besides, he likes working by himself.

He drives in from the suburbs weekdays at 6 a.m., gets to the shop and throws a few waste sticks of deodar cedar into the woodstove to nip the early morning chill. The wood is so fragrant it smells almost like cologne. He eats his own homemade granola topped with banana and papaya, drinks aged Indonesian decaf, reads the paper, pets Minou, then starts work.

Today, work is a four-panel door that he will make with stiles and rails of Douglas fir, panels of Central African bubinga and moldings of East Indian rosewood. Peter salvaged the fir from a company that was getting rid of 45-year-old wooden pickling vats the size of brewery tanks. The outside of the vats' 3-inch-thick beams was mealy and had to be planed off, but the pickled side was hard and fine. Peter bought the rippled pink bubinga heartwood 15 years ago for what seemed then like an outrageous price. Today, bubinga this magnificent is hard to find at any price. The rosewood, a purple-tinged variety that he loves, has been knocking around the shop for years, waiting for the right door. This is the right door because Peter is making it for his own house, which he plans to build by himself as soon as he finds the right piece of land. No, he doesn't think he'll need help. He'll erect walls with rope-and-pulley contraptions, lug beams on dollies, hike posts with jacks and levers. He'll build the cabinets and do the woodwork – alone.

He began working alone decades ago. After graduating from Cornell University, as had his father before him, he did a stint in the U.S. Army and eventually graduated from Berkeley's architecture school. The job market was then glutted with young architects, so Peter promptly became unemployed. As an architecture student, he had learned a lot about designing buildings but practically nothing about constructing them. Still, he landed a job building a house addition for a married couple. He designed an unusual five-walled living room, and the owners loved it. So Peter went down to the lumberyard and found a man who agreed to tell him how to build his distinctively designed room in return for buying his supplies at the store.

"What are you making it out of?" the man asked.

"What do you suggest?" Peter asked back, only partially in jest.

But Peter was a natural. He had built elaborate tree houses as a kid. At 14, he had turned a branching tree trunk into a pedestal desk. As a teenager, he had wired a neighbor's house. He was the kind of kid who built his own radios from scratch, who had a complete collection of *National Geographic* magazines dating back to 1913. He had put himself through Berkeley repairing IBM typewriters, every year winning the company's local speed repair championship. But IBM wasn't the place for him. "I always felt as if I were trapped in a giant machine. When I left home in the morning, I left my true personality behind. It never felt right." The five-walled room turned out rather well – and decades later Peter and the couple still trade Christmas cards. He stumbled into door making. A customer couldn't find doors he liked, so Peter made a pair of simple doors built of redwood cast on the diagonal. One of the man's friends saw the doors and asked him to build him a door. Then came another friend. And another.

"Well," Peter told himself, "I guess I'm in the door business."

That was 500 doors ago.

"I've built some pretty unusual doors," he says. He once built a fir door with hidden wooden panels that could be raised to hide its windows for a couple who traveled a lot and wanted extra security while they were away. He made 10 mahogany four-panel doors with each panel rimmed in a solid brass frame that could be removed for cleaning so the brass polish wouldn't damage the wood. He made a wooden door with lower panels of steel painted to look like wood to keep a family's Doberman pinschers from scratching the door to splinters.

"A custom door to me is a door based on someone's wild idea," Peter says. "It's often not just a door." People have commissioned his doors because they want to recreate a favorite castle door from their English childhoods, because they are re-clusive and want a door that blends into the wall and cannot be seen by uninvited visitors, because in their home they want to enshrine timber they have salvaged from a railroad trestle they played on as children. One man wasn't so concerned about the way his door was going to look as he was obsessed with the way it was going to feel. As a boy, the man had had a silky-feeling piece of furniture in his room. When he touched his new door, he wanted that sensation rekindled. So Peter made sample fin-ishes until the man said, "Oh, that feels just like it."

People who commission a Peter Good door often want it to be a kind of story about themselves. Translating the story a customer breathes into his idea of a door is a big part of Pe-ter's job. Unlike an artist who thinks of his work only as self-ex-pression, Peter aims to express the customer's vision. Sure, it's good business. But it's more than that. A craftsman is like a writer struggling to tell someone else's story, a painter com-mitted to rendering someone else's dream. To Peter, it is im-moral to talk a customer into a door he doesn't really want, to convince him that mahogany is the right wood simply because Peter has a pile of mahogany back at the shop. Peter's job is to discern the customer's vision. The human artistry in crafts-manship, after mastering tools and materials, he says, is in the union of one person's vision and another person's implementa-tion of that vision.

"That's why I never get attached to my doors. I've put up some doors that I thought were the ugliest doors on the face of the earth. But they were not my doors. The pleasure is having a door turn out the way I visualized it." He knows he has suc-ceeded when a customer says, "That's exactly what I wanted."

People always want to know if anyone else will be work-ing on their doors. They want to make sure their handmade story isn't tainted with assembly-line techniques. "Let me put it this way," Peter tells them. "If I drop dead in the middle of this job, you won't get your door." People want to know stories about the building of their doors, including all the little flaws that make them distinctive, even stories about how Peter nicked his finger in the cutting of a stile or caught a splinter in the sanding of a rail. "It's almost like people take comfort in knowing I suffered a bit in making their doors."

Some craftsmen become cynical about affluent customers desperate to transfer the distinctiveness of objects to themselves, as if clothes made the man. Not Peter. His customers' desires have allowed him to achieve not only what his customers crave but also what he himself has spent much of his life seeking: to write his own singular story in this cookie-cutter age. He nods to the boards of Douglas fir, the bubinga panels, the rosewood moldings that are about to become a door. "Nobody else has ever made this door. Nobody has ever seen this door. I'll create something that wasn't there before, something that has never existed. And I'll do it all myself. I like that. It has become part of who I am."

Peter has talked way too much today, always turning from the table saw or router or sander as he does, interrupting the work. But even with talking, he has cut his wood to size and sawed the 2-inch mortises and tenons in the strong outside frame of the door and the 1-inch mortises and tenons in the pieces that will compose the door's interior works. He has run 24 6-foot lengths of 1×1 rosewood through the router four times with four different bits to get the molding profile he wants. The rosewood leavings smell like cinnamon. He has taken a splinter in the first knuckle of his left index finger. He has dry-fitted the door, disassembled it and brushed the joints with plastic resin glue. He has put the door back together, hammered its joints tight and clamped them in place, leaving it ready to be sanded and varnished. He has done all of this through a haze of sawdust that reflects hazily in the workshop's pale fluorescent light.

"The work's hard and dirty. The fact remains: I like it."

Peter recently visited Ritzville, Washington, and as he walked past the local wheat growers' association headquarters, he had a thought. When he got home, he bought 300 tiny neon bulbs that he plans to embed in stalks of wheat carved into a wooden door. "Don't you think a wheat growers' board should have wheat on its door?" The ideas never stop. There's the door to Rick's Café Américain in the movie *Casablanca*. "Wow, nice door!" Peter once told his wife in the middle of watching the film. "I'd like to build it someday." And he'd like to build a door made of stone... and a door that would open like the budding iris diaphragm in a camera lens... and a faux door that someday, if he lives long enough, could be projected as a hologram creating a door that is not actually there.

"I love doors," he says. "Doors are what I do."

TWELVE

TEDD BENSON

THE CRAFT OF CRAFTSMANSHIP

The leaden clunk-clunk of work boots on the long pier carries farther than Tedd Benson can see this morning, just after dawn, in the thick fog off the coast of Mystic, Connecticut. Accompanied by his friend and coworker, Andrew Dey, he drops his tool belt into a white skiff, climbs in, steadies himself and releases the mooring lines. Soon, the boat is churning blindly through the silence and dead-calm water on its way to Dodge Island, where still another of Tedd's famous timber frame houses will rise in skeletal elegance this morning. It has been decades since Tedd erected his first timber frame – giant wooden posts and beams interlocked with joints and wooden pegs and braces – and sparked the revival of a 2,000-year-old tradition that had been nearly lost in the United States. His 1980 book, *Building the Timber Frame House*, made him a cult figure thanks to its almost religious respect for a craft that had created ancient Greek and Japanese temples, Scandinavian stave churches, Colonial meeting houses and other buildings that have survived the ages. Tedd's company has added 300 timber frame houses to the legacy, but he's still wistful about the one that started it all.

"When my first timber frame went up," he says, "the feeling I had must have been what a cathedral builder felt standing beneath his magnificent structure. You're humbled by your own creation, this building that will stand for 500 years. You feel small and big at once – big for having accomplished it, small in relation to it. And that feeling is what keeps me and all craftsmen doing it every day. There's nothing romantic about sweating over these grungy, dirty old timbers. But seeing that building go up, well, it can make you cry."

Andrew, the manager of the Dodge Island project, who is steering the skiff this morning, says, "The timbers look great. We had a lot of cleaning up to do after getting 'em off the barge."

"How's your leg?" Tedd asks, looking toward the bandage that covers a deep gash in Andrew's left calf.

"It's fine."

"Take care of it."

Andrew nods but doesn't answer.

These days, Andrew and the 31 other men and women of Benson Woodworking know they can get along fine without the boss's advice. And that's exactly the way Tedd wants it, because his mission now is to create a working environment where others can also get the feeling he first had so many houses ago. For years, Benson has pondered whatever ineffable thing it is that moves men and women to do their best work, to blend obsessive attention to detail with creativity, to make people love what they do despite tedious, repetitive labor. He has concluded that skill alone doesn't make excellence, not in its highest form, anyway. No, excellence is a state of mind. "It's a way of thinking," he says. "A way of being."

Dodge Island is tiny, really a stone's throw wide. But on this speck of land that is like a head held hopefully just above the water is a clearing where the $1.1 million, 4,200-square-foot house of David Elliman and Andrea Branch will stand. Its rear windows will face Mystic, its front windows will face a distant lighthouse and, beyond, the Atlantic.

At 7:58 a.m., with fog still shrouding the shoreline, the smell of brackish water mingles with that of citrus oil freshly spread on timbers. Saws and drills, clamps and tool chests are scattered helter-skelter, and a crane huffs and puffs like a snorting bull. The frame of the house is stacked in four huge skeletal walls lying atop one another on the foundation in the order in which they will be raised by the crane. The top beams – the plates – of two walls are 72 feet long and 12 by 14 inches thick. The walls were pieced together and pegged on-site in a build-by-number system: Vertical timber posts were lettered A, B, C and on through the alphabet from the front to the back of the house; the horizontal girt, summer and joist beams were marked by their first- or second-floor numbers; the sides of all timbers were labeled north, south, east and west.

The elaborate joinery, which resembles furniture-making done by a race of giants, is a triumph of geometric couplings named not in the vocabulary of mathematics but in the plain language of poetry, history or, perhaps, Shaker song: Simple mortise and tenon joints to carry a light load, shouldered joints to bear great weight, anchor-beam joints borrowed from the barns of the Pennsylvania Dutch, spline joints from the Japanese, scarf joints from the medieval Europeans, plus dovetail, rafter feet bird's-mouth, tusk tenon, collar-tie and tongue-and-fork joints. The timbers were cut to length and planed to width at Tedd's shop in the woods near Alstead Center, New Hampshire. Joints were sketched on the timbers and, in a kind of woodworker's hieroglyphics, directions were scrawled for those who will saw and bore the hundreds of housings and couplings.

"Clean the pockets!"

On Dodge Island, raising foreman Mark Roentsch yells out the order as the first wall hangs from the crane and sways gently, looking weightless a few inches above the foundation deck mortises into which its vertical posts will slide. Hand-guided into the pockets by seven men and seated, the wall is plumbed and braced.

"Home!" Mark hollers, and the wall is up.

Tedd stands to the side of the foundation, obscured by the huge gray boulders that litter the island, a tourist among workmen hustling to install diagonal knee braces where wall timbers meet at right angles. Forty-eight years old, tall, with blond-to-gray hair and an athletic build, he looks calm, but he's itching to grab a beetle – a 15-pound wooden mallet for tapping joints together – and put in a few swings, use the old muscles, rub the old emotions. Instead, he stands with his arms planted on his hips, watching.

"One day about six years ago, I was inside the shop in the morning and a couple of men came shuffling in late. It hit me like a rock: Here are these men I have worked with for years, who I care for, and they don't want to be here. This craft we had committed our lives to wasn't enough, not for them. That day, I looked around and noticed others doing the same – just not giving 100 percent. The next day, I said, 'I'm leaving. Something's not right about our workplace. I'm assuming it's me.'"

For two months, Tedd stayed home and read books on management. And, indeed, he decided he was the problem: After 18 years in business, he had become a control freak. "I was the aperture through which everything had to pass." It slowed projects to a crawl and left workers twiddling their thumbs waiting for Tedd, who was working 17-hour days, flying to construction sites, taking late-night calls. Clearly, he needed to delegate. But he saw that as a surface problem, a wave atop the ocean. Sure, he could create a new layer of managers – several new apertures through which every decision would pass. That would unclog the system. But it didn't seem right, not for the work he and his team did.

Instead, Tedd thought back to when he was a young, smart, counterculture college dropout from Colorado who'd worked on house-framing crews, banging 16-penny nails into 2 × 4 studs, expected by his bosses to rip through the work, putting nothing of himself into it – bored. He moved to New England and met Oliver Chase, a sixth-generation banger of nails, Harvard educated, a man who built houses not to make a living but because he loved it.

"Oliver would say, 'Our civilization is defined by what we make. It's a privilege to be a part of that tradition.' He looked for the challenges – understanding how a framing square works. It's an old layout tool that's just a right angle, but with it you can lay out rafters and stairs, octagons and polygons. I'd never worked with anybody who used a square other than to draw a line on a board."

"Home!" Mark Roentsch suddenly hollers again.

And at 8:27, the second wall is up.

During his self-imposed leave of absence, Tedd thought back to the early timber frame houses he had built, thought back to that feeling – his excitement at locking a giant dovetail joint for the first time, seeing the last purlin go into a roof. "It was so exciting that it seems as if it happened in a dream." In those days, he worked for the thrill of it, the chance to stand within the finished cathedral and feel that amazing, purifying wash of pride and humility. That was the emotional rush, the heart of his craft.

"Push on three!" Mark yells. "One, two, three…"

At 9:06, the crane growls, the third wall dangles lightly in the air and the yellow and purple ropes that hold it are now bright in the first rays of the sun burning through the mist.

"Home!" Mark cries.

Suddenly, Tedd can't wait on the sidelines anymore. When the crane's cable jams, he grabs a giant sledge and swings with a force that clang-clangs like a ship's bell. When the cable is free, he stretches, rolls his shoulders, looks energized. Soon, he's up a ladder atop a 72-foot-long plate, a cat on dexterous paws. He unties a rope, lets it fall, sits astride the beam. In the thinning fog is now revealed not only the distant lighthouse but also a flotilla of small boats presumably investigating what's up on Dodge Island.

"Ready!" Mark hollers.

At 11:15, the crane begins to lift the slack on the ropes now attached to the last wall.

"One, two, three…"

When Tedd returned to work six years ago, after those two months off, he had decided he was robbing his workers of the juice, sapping the joy in their work, draining their motivation. He was holding the hands of architects and designers, choosing what joints to use where, orchestrating raisings – getting the rush and taking the praise of clients. So he stepped back. Although Benson Woodworking usually has three or four crews out working on houses at any given time, Tedd stopped visiting sites regularly. He even chose not to attend most raisings.

"I had become a hog for that feeling," he says. "Maybe I was a junkie. I was robbing the people who worked for me. They needed that feeling, too." Benson told his workers they must run the company. He would concentrate on the big picture, where Benson Woodworking would go in the future. His workers set up committees to review hiring and pay raises. Everyone found out what everyone else in the company was earning. Each employee shared in annual profits. Jobs, from best to worst, rotated among shop workers: One day a worker oversees a million-dollar project, the next day he butt-cuts timber and sweeps the floor. "No craftsman ever built a timber frame by himself," Tedd says. "It always takes at least two people to carry the timber."

Back at the shop in Alstead Center, for instance, men are doing for other buildings what was done long ago for the Dodge Island house. Amid the scent of white-pine timbers, Tom Hancock is running the mortise-cutting machine, a boring job. But he has just finished managing the construction of a million-dollar building and soon will take his family to see his achievement. Ryosei Kaneko, a craftsman from Japan, is jotting directions on timbers for a $150,000 house, using his trig calculator to figure its compound joints. Afterward, he will sweep the floor. Meanwhile, Robert Polcari is hand-routing mortises on the timbers of a $300,000 house's roof, which, according to the calculations he makes on his framing square, will rise 10 inches diagonally for every 12 inches of horizontal run. In the ancient language of the framing square, he calls the roof's 39.8-degree tilt "a 10/12 pitch" – just as Oliver Chase would have done. Later, Robert Polcari, too, will sweep the floor.

On Dodge Island, others are also carrying the timber. Paul Boa, a quiet, meticulous master woodworker, is a stickler for process, always making sure each step is taken in sequence. Mark Roentsch hates too much process. "Enough," he'll say. "Let's go do it." And there's Andrew Dey, the boat-driving project manager with the gashed leg, a Harvard graduate, who loves to bang nails but who can talk to affluent clients with reassuring sophistication.

"Making a crew is like a recipe," says Tedd, who has now climbed down from the heights and stepped back among the boulders, anticipating the reaction of the home's owners, who have just arrived. "It's the craft of making craftsmanship."

There's still much more to do. The perpendicular beams that link the raised walls must be installed, the roof trusses lifted and locked, the purlins that connect them beetled into their dovetails, the siding, insulation, wiring, plumbing, heating and flooring, all of which present unique problems in timber frames, must be installed – at least another nine months of work.

But these details are part of the mechanics of craftsmanship, the grungy, dirty work it took to get to this place: In a few moments, Tedd knows the emotional rush will flow, as the awestruck owners will praise the craftsmen, who will be standing beneath their creation feeling that affirming wash of pride and humility. Off among the boulders, Tedd doesn't want to be with them. This cathedral he did not build. Of the feeling, he says, "I miss it a lot."

At 11:27, Mark cries, "Cable down!"

"Clean the pockets!"

"Home!"

And the final wall is up.

THIRTEEN

MANUEL PALOS

THE DRAGON
IN THE STONE

The client looked pretty seedy in a baseball cap and torn pants, his head canted gawkily off kilter. But when he first walked into Manuel Palos's San Francisco workshop, it wasn't the man who caught the sculptor's eye – it was the woman with him. "She was stunningly beautiful," says Manuel, his English blending with his native Mexican Spanish and his acquired Italian, his sentences made distinctive by accents placed on normally unaccented words and syllables, as in: "She *was* stun*ning*ly beau*ti*ful." Manuel was at a large, low table where he always keeps a dozen sculptures in progress, edging the muscle in a woman's calf or shaping the eyebrow on a boy's face. He let go of the trigger of his pneumatic hammer, and its wheezing halted. In his odd accent, he asked, "What *can* I *do* for *you?*

"I want something on top of my fireplace like a serpent or a dragon," the man said in a deep, languid voice. Manuel, figuring him for a kook, decided to play a teasing game.

"I got a better idea," he said. "Why don't I make you a huge dragon, and the fireplace will be his mouth?" Aiming to shock – and certain that this would end the game – he added that the job would cost $60,000 to $70,000.

"Mr. Palos, here's a $10,000 deposit," the man said, handing him a check, and left. Taken aback, Manuel hurried to his office and asked his secretary to see if the man had that much money in his account. She glanced at the check.

"This is Nicolas Cage," she said. "The famous actor." The teasing had turned.

Oh, no, Manuel thought, *so now I have to come up with my joke.*

Years later, as Manuel Palos tells this story on a Sunday morning, the pneumatic hammer wheezes and stone dust billows around him in his 7,000-square-foot workshop. The dragon that now frames Cage's fireplace – a fierce and magnificent 10-by-13-foot creature carved from 4 1/2 tons of black Mexican limestone – is only one of many of his monumental stone carvings and cement castings in San Francisco. His eight 13-foot-tall eagles look as if they might fly off the top of the Pacific Telephone building. His 9-foot-high Greek gods – Zeus and Medusa among them – adorn the Palace of the Legion of Honor. His fountains and fireplaces decorate the lobbies of the Villa Florence and Galleria Park hotels.

"I am so lucky," says Manuel, who at age 60 likes to work alone in his shop every weekend, away from the normal workday distractions. "Very few sculptors have the satisfaction to have their work in public and lit up all night like my eagles. Even the Greeks and Romans didn't have their sculptures lit up all night – no electricity! I really enjoy my life. There are people who are born to be something and who find out early enough to enjoy the rest of their lives doing what they want. That's the trick."

Manuel is seated before a chunk of French limestone he is carving into a noble lion that will sit as one of the pedestals beneath the jambs of a 1,500-pound $25,000 fireplace in a house on San Francisco's Postcard Row. In his right hand, he tightly grips the air hammer's nozzle. The fingertips of his left hand hold the pencil-size chisel bit while he turns the bit like a spindle to etch the loops of the lion's billowing mane. Manuel leans into his work, his weight on the toes of his right foot. His right arm, which has carved stone for 30 years, is much stronger than his left. He wears a teal beret.

"This is how it is done, and – oh, God – it is fun!" he says, leaning back and letting the air hammer whine down. "I love to work. What a gift! It's bringing life to the lion. My father used to say, 'Do your best.' He didn't know anything about art, but he was an artist. He was the best shoemaker in Tabasco, Mexico."

Manuel immigrated to San Francisco as a young man looking for work. He became a U.S. citizen and began laboring in an architectural ornament company. He met old men – of Irish, German and Italian heritage –who had spent their lives sculpting clay models for castings and carving stone window and door arches, cornices, corbels and columns, fountains and fireplaces. In the old days, the sons of these men would have learned their fathers' craft, but no more. "They wanted to go to college, go work in a bank," Manuel says. "The men had so much to teach and didn't have anybody to teach it to."

So the old men taught Manuel. They taught him to stand back from a stone as he carved to better see the grand sweep of his work. They taught him to work on one piece, then another, then return to the first. The lapsed time let the work simmer in the mind and eye, revealing flaws more readily. They taught him to lean on the toes of his right foot as he carved and to swing the hammer not only with his arm and wrist but also with his whole body, like a boxer who throws a right hook from the balls of his feet through his torso and arm and out his fist, hitting his mark 2 or 3 inches from his arm's full extension.

It drove Manuel crazy that the old men insisted on listening to classical music while they worked. "Well, in about two months," he says, "I couldn't work without classical music. And now I know why. It relaxes. That music has been created with discipline. It is so well done that it lasts forever. Anything well done lasts forever." The old men convinced Manuel that he had to study in Italy, famous for stone carving. So he began spending two months every summer in Carrara, where Michelangelo cut the marble for his Pieta. Manuel's first wife couldn't abide his obsession, thought he was crazy. She wanted him to work on a city garbage truck. Why not? Good pay, insurance, vacations, retirement. Instead, at 33, he quit his job and launched his own casting and carving business. Even the old men told him it was too risky.

"I was starving," Manuel says, "but I never thought about doing it to make money. It was something in me waiting to come out. I felt compelled to let it go." By then, work had become his life. "Having your work under control, the rest of your life falls into place. Your friends and family have respect for you. And then you feel that respect too."

All around him in his workshop this morning is proof of respect deserved: the fireplace he is carving with its roaring lion pedestals and its ancient Irish warriors standing erect, carrying the mantel upon their heads; castings of the giant eagle and the Greek gods; a bowl-shaped mold the size of a spaceship that will be cast as a mansion's oval ceiling; Doric columns, cornices and capitals. In the center of the room, on the large, low table, sit the marble busts and bodies he carves just for pleasure.

"I am so, so lucky," he says, again.

The air hammer wheezes, and Manuel leans on his toes and into his work. He is refining the lion, working with a three-toed 3/8-inch chisel bit and gentle air power, digging between the curls of the mane to make the tresses jump out in relief. Later, he will run a sharp, delicate bit over the sculpture's entire surface to remove the crosshatching toe marks left by the rough-cutting chisels. Except for the air hammer, which has cut carving time 10-fold over hammer-and-chisel work, stone carving is much as it was centuries ago.

The rough stone must be skinned by driving a 2 1/2-pound hammer onto the head of a 10-inch carbide-steel-tipped chisel held loosely so that it will ride with the natural grain. After skinning, the carver draws in the stone, starting with bigger chisels and more air power to rough out his design. He then progressively works his way down to smaller bits and less force, until he's where Manuel is today. The fireplace – with its lion manes, snarling mouths, paws, muscles and sinew; its warrior faces, beards, teeth, eyes, ears and helmets; its garlands, acanthus leaves and flower buds – has taken two months of work. Smoothing its surface and sharpening its details will take Manuel two more weeks.

"It's not all inspiration," he says. "It's work, dedication."

Manuel works on a 6-by-6-inch square of mane for an hour, getting it perfect. Then, still following the advice of the old men who taught him, he leaves the lion to simmer in his mind and eye, moves across his workshop and leans into a small marble bust of a young girl that is emerging from an 8-by-8-inch block of pink marble that Manuel shipped home from Italy. "You'll think I'm crazy, but I look at her, and I see a smile, a little smile." The stone only hints at the girl's face now, as if it were shrouded in tomb cloth. But in a few minutes, Manuel has drawn a chin and shaped a cheek. He then works on the smile that only he can see.

"Three hundred years ago," he says, "there was no room for sloppiness or 'that's good enough.' Well done was perfect." And that is what Manuel hopes to approach, although he believes that many clients don't know the difference between mediocrity and near perfection. And, he says, the financial pressure to cut corners is great. He once took a job carving a monument for a California town and underestimated the time it would take. He told the town fathers that he would end up losing $20,000 because of the extra time needed to finish the monument to his satisfaction. "I will have to do it for free," he told them, "but I will have to do it." To his relief, the town fathers paid the extra money.

He spits on the girl's marble cheek, rubs off the gray dust with his fingertips – and suddenly her skin shines pink and bright with a subtle white grain radiating through it. Manuel is elated. It is a thrill that, even after 30 years of carving, is fresh every time. He believes it has something to do with touching the wonder of creation. A decade ago, he was in Italy, working on a woman's torso in Portuguese marble. As he carved, he realized he would not have enough stone for the left breast. In an instant, without conscious thought, Manuel dug into the stone and indented the breast as a reverse image, to the later amazement and awe of his fellow carvers. "I felt like I had an extra gift that God gave me to create that beauty," he says. That wonder has never faded and, when he looks at the torso today, he still thinks, "How did I do that?"

Manuel feels the same awe about Nicolas Cage's dragon. He went to Mexico to select 13 giant pieces of limestone.

He drove the truck that carried the stone back to San Francisco, where he began carving the dragon's fiery mouth and fangs, then moved up to its flared nostrils and evil eyes. It took six months. But, as Manuel says, anything well done lasts forever. And sometimes he ponders a time 200, 300, 1,000 years from now when San Francisco may lie in ruins... yet rising forth will be his dragon. What will they make of it? A giant talisman? A rendering of God? Or the devil? An altar for sacrifice? Perhaps Nicolas Cage's fancy and Manuel Palos's joke will turn out to be a mysterious Stonehenge from our time.

This morning, Manuel will work on the girl's face a while longer, until anyone who looks will see her smile. Then he will return to the lion's mane or to the faces of the Irish soldiers of his fireplace – or to the sitting woman, the turbaned head or the muscled back he sees in several pieces of still uncarved marble.

"I want to someday die happy with my sculpture and remember how I did it all," he says. "Resting is not enough for me. I have to keep carving, keep carving."

FOURTEEN

PETER KING

GOD MADE MAN
OUT OF CLAY

"Peter," says Katie Smead, "I'd like you to dedicate my kiln."

The request takes Peter King by surprise. After a long day in his architectural ceramics workshop in Pensacola, Florida, he is exhausted from slaking, milling, pounding, rolling, laying out, scoring and sculpting 700 pounds of clay that will eventually become a glazed wall of rising and falling ocean waves. The last few days, Peter has been pondering why he is so obsessed, so in love with a craft that has paid him so little in money. Tonight, after a glass of wine, he has been thinking about this again, absently rubbing his tired eyes, tugging at his beard and stroking his ponytail as the 30 or so men and women who have come to celebrate the first batch of pottery fired in Katie's new backyard kiln mingle around him. Katie is a novice ceramicist who studied under Peter. So he feigns energy and laughs his quick Gatling-gun laugh: "Ha. Ha. Ha."

"Sure," he tells her. "Be glad to."

Soon, to oohs and aahs, people are removing a score of flame-hot handmade pots, bowls and cups from the kiln. Off by himself, Peter, a thin man in shorts and a casual flowered shirt, has noticed that the points of the early evening's quarter moon are tilted to five minutes after 7. A cooling wind blows from the east. But when it stops, the muggy Florida air presses like an overcoat on his skin. The humidity reminds him of a scene from *One Hundred Years of Solitude* in which it has rained for four years and, Gabriel Garcia Marquez writes, the "air was so damp that fish could have come in through the doors and swum out the windows." Peter would like to go home, read a few pages of Garcia Marquez and fall asleep. Instead, he thinks:

What will I say to dedicate Katie's kiln?

Peter King, 46 years old, has been making ceramics for 25 years, taking plain clay, shaping it with his hands and tools and firing it until it is as hard and strong as brick. Like Katie, he began with pots but then moved on to floor tiles, fireplaces, door frames, gateways, entire walls. In college, on his way

to a philosophy degree, he and a friend wandered into a potter's studio. "I remember seeing that first pot being turned on
a wheel," he says. "I became addicted." He finished his degree
but abandoned plans for graduate school. Instead, he spent up
to 20 hours a day in the studio. And once, at 4 in the morning
as he massaged wet clay in his hands, he had a waking dream:
"I envisioned these huge ceramic columns, and I went, 'You
could really make anything out of this stuff.'"

It was an oddly prescient thought for a 21-year-old kid
with no knowledge of architectural history, no idea that Bab-
ylon's Ishtar Gate was a ceramic mural, that the Incas of Peru
decorated temples with ceramics, that – before the 20th century's stark industrial architecture – ceramic pillars, cornices and
arches often adorned buildings in the United States and Europe. For years, Peter made coffee cups and flowerpots and sold
them out of an old van at craft shows on the East Coast. Then
one day he was talking with a man for whom he was making a
ceramic sink. The man said he was putting in a new fireplace –
and Peter, on a whim, offered to build it out of clay: 10 feet high,
6 feet wide, in a simple art-deco seashell design. He laughs at
the memory: "It was an overnight conversion."

Since then, his StoneHaus studio in Pensacola has pro-
duced hundreds of one-of-a-kind ceramic architectural adornments. He calls his work "clay carpentry"—Spanish, Pueblo and
Gothic arches, ocean-wave wainscoting, Mayan baseboards, a
fountain that mimics a pipe organ, a door protected by a giant African shield, multicolored garden gates 15 feet high and fireplaces
with Aztec birds, Italianate shells, Jacobean columns, flamingos,
great blue herons, dolphins, palm trees, every imaginable flying
fish, Egyptian hieroglyphs, dragons, geometric concoctions, even
human faces. Someone pours Peter another glass of wine.

He thinks, *So what will I say tonight?*

Peter has been moody lately, ruminating to himself about
his work. "I'm well past 40, and I still haven't made any money,"
he says. "I owe $30,000 on my credit card." He works seven

days a week and lives in three rooms over his shop. He drives an old Ford van with an odometer turning 170,000 miles. His yearning for affluence constantly collides with his stubborn perfectionism. For instance, he once agreed to charge $50,000 to build elaborate gates for a sculpture park in Maryland. He belatedly realized his gates were too small for the setting—he made them 2 feet wider and 2 feet taller. After the fix, he lost $15,000.

"I couldn't put that piece out there and have it be less when it could be more. If I don't make money, that's all right. There is an ineffable thing about each piece of work when you know it's right no matter what anyone says." People so obsessed with excellence are often said to take pride in their work. That's too simple. Pride isn't the source of his excellence, Peter says. Pride is instead a product of doing something as close to per-fectly as he can: "It is an indescribable feeling. It's not because others say it's great. It's internal. The Bible says man was made in the image of God. That doesn't mean He has two arms and two legs. It means that, like for God, the most important thing we do is create. It's deep in us, somewhere near the brain stem. When I finally get a piece on the wall, it's there: a physical enti-ty. It was once an idea, and now it won't go away. I made stone out of my fingertips. That kind of power is seductive.

"That's why God made man out of clay."

Peter creates entire fireplaces and walls of red clay in a cramped, dim garage workshop. He and two workers start with 100-pound clay slabs 48 inches long, 30 inches wide and 1 inch thick, laying the slabs on giant wheeled tables that creak and moan under the clay's weight like a house settling on its foundation. The men use blades, chopsticks, hair combs and the tips of their fingers to etch drawings and patterns into silky clay hand-dug from an abandoned pit nearby. When sculpting three-dimensional birds, fish, waves or abstract shapes, the men layer up to 5 inches of clay in relief. While still soft, the huge sculptures are cut into pieces and numbered, then left to dry for two to six weeks before being sanded with 60-grit paper and painted with chemical glazes. Melted in a walk-in kiln heated to 2,300 degrees Fahrenheit, the glazes create a flower garden of colors and textures. The fired pieces are hauled to the site and secured by industrial epoxy and hidden screws. Peter can make about 10 architectural pieces a year.

"Going full bore, that's all we can do."

He knows potters who find marketable lines of objects and then stick to them, build reputations, mass-produce and earn good livings. He respects them. He just can't do it. Some of his passion for work he learned from his dad, a milkman who could make anything with his hands. Some of it grows from the sensation of clay in his palms – the cool, lush softness that has smoothed his fingerprints over the years. And some of it comes from the glee he takes in knowing he has turned child's play into a job, while others must always beware the boss. But the passion goes deeper too.

"I can't stop," he says. "It's sheer compulsion. Any master craftsman is seeking something. In that sense, it's a religious quest: 'I have to do this myself.' Yes, you have to develop the skills to meet the challenges of material and environment, but a lot of people do that. Master craftsmen aren't making objects, not really. They are looking to find something in themselves. They will always want to do a little bit more." They don't measure accomplishment against the finished work, Peter says, but against the past intensity of feeling inside themselves each time they have created an object, whether a fireplace, a chair, a door or a house.

"That's the source, the wellspring."

The battle, Peter says, is balancing perfectionism with the economics of getting the job done. "You can be so perfectionist that you can't make anything." He smiles, laughs and asks, "Why did God say, 'This is good' on Saturday after he made man? What he really meant was, 'This is good enough. I'm going home. Tomorrow is Sunday.'"

Tonight, as darkness falls on him and his friends, Peter is satisfied that an abstract fireplace he finished last week is good enough. The 14-foot-tall fireplace is a collection of fragments: broken bricks and clay pots meant to look like archaeological remnants, Indian wood-block designs pressed willy-nilly into the clay, imprints from a scrap of burlap and a piece of lace, grout smoothed in seams, grout rough and sloppy in seams, glazed spots reflecting the sunlight, unglazed spots as dull as dry mud.

Already, Peter's obsession with always enhancing his last creation has kicked in. If he could remake the fireplace, he would go with a much drier-looking surface, less dancing light and more color – deep turquoise, matte lavender and the bright lavenders of a Florida sunset. "I always know what a piece could have been," he says, "and that haunts me." The indescribably good feeling he gets in the making must be topped in the next job, or he will be disappointed.

So, how to dedicate Katie's kiln?

Well, he certainly won't reveal the thoughts that have been swirling around in his head the last few days. Too dreary. It's a party not a philosophical retreat on how creativity and mastery of craft intertwine, not a spirit quest into the source of hard work and pride and inspiration, not a seminar on the modern craftsman zeitgeist. Hell, it's a party! A ring has appeared around the moon. To cool off, Peter has rolled his ponytail into a knob at the nape of his neck. Everyone is now pawing Katie's pottery, which has cooled enough to be lifted and turned and studied in the vague backyard light.

"Beautiful!"

"Wonderful!"

"Look at this!"

Katie stands before the empty open kiln and says loudly enough for all to hear, "I've asked Peter to dedicate my kiln." He stands next to her, caught in a frozen pose with his weight on his right heel, holding his glass in his right hand at his waist, stroking his beard with his left hand. He looks at the ground, doesn't speak. People go quiet, then uncomfortably quiet. He finally looks up, his face and his eyes still tired, and decides, after all, to tell them something of what has been on his mind.

"People ask me why I do what I do. I make very little money. Why not create a line of pottery that I can mass-produce and make a decent living? Well, tonight is the reason why I don't. Each time I or Katie or anyone makes a piece of pottery, it's a reach for doing it more perfectly. Each piece is like Athena bursting from the head of Zeus – it is an idea coming forth from your own head. And it's that sensation that keeps us going.

"I know people who retire early with a lot of money. They think of their lives in distinct pieces – make money young and be really unhappy and then retire and play golf the rest of their lives. I can't understand those people. If I were to win the lottery tomorrow, I'd still do exactly what I do today. What I do is who I am. It's not a job. It's who I am.

"A friend once told me that making a ceramic piece is the work of mother earth and father fire and whoever is doing the making. It is that confluence of material and creativity that makes the object. So here, tonight, we celebrate mother earth, father fire – and Katie."

Suddenly, Peter gulps down his wine like a shot of vodka, spins and, in a wide sweeping stroke, throws and smashes his glass inside Katie's new kiln.

"To mother earth, father fire—and Katie!"

EPILOGUE

WHEN WORK IS WORSHIP

So, back to the beginning...

Why did my best friends from high school and college and the country boy who renovated my house love to drive screws, pound nails and cut boards, but I didn't? I think it's because I never lingered long enough over a job to discover that the journey should have been my destination. I never swung a hammer at a piece of copper long enough to witness the inanimate come to life—not copper, not iron, not wood, not clay. I saw the work as a nasty means to an end: I labored for money, a bigger house, a nicer bathroom, as did many in *Acts of Creation* before their moments of emotional, even spiritual, conversion at the joy of *doing* the work.

Fine craftsmen don't work only to get done, to get paid. They work in the moment. They work for a *feeling* that is rare and beautiful and ineffable. Wanting that *feeling* again and again drives and inspires them. I understand, all right. I get paid to write, but I don't write only to get paid. Remember, I can fiddle with five pages of writing all day long and feel refreshed at the end, feel as if only minutes have passed, as if I have added something of value to the world. One craft caught me, one craft didn't. I went my way. My friends went theirs.

Yet, we all recognize one another when we meet and nod in tacit acknowledgment at the shared wonder of it—the sliver of craftsmen, writers, doctors, teachers, lawyers, artists, athletes, plumbers, factory workers, shop owners, CEOs, actors, electricians, scientists, song writers and handymen who, for whatever reasons, crave the exhilaration of touching excellence every day in their work. They can't understand anyone who doesn't. As Tedd Benson says: *It is a way of being.*

We understand the words of...

American poet Donald Hall: "Work survives the worker."

Mythologist Joseph Campbell: "Follow your bliss."

Scottish philosopher Thomas Carlyle: "Work is worship."

We have never said: "Thank God it's Friday."

And we thank God for that.

If you have read this far, you are one who understands.

Amen.

ACKNOWLEDGMENTS

These articles would never have been done without the militant support of Steve Petranek, the former editor of *This Old House Magazine*. He loved the idea of doing not how-to or informational profiles of fine craftsmen but stories about how their creativity informed their craft and their creations. He had a consultant who thought the stories were, well, kind of weird. But he resisted and paid me, along with footing the substantial travel bills, to keep going. Steve's second in command, the boundlessly talented David Grogan, did the hands-on editing of the articles and improved each story immensely—from word-by-word enhancements to helping sort out the big ideas that were running silently through the stories as they came and went. Working with two so brilliant men was a highlight of my long career. Special thanks to agent Sloan Harris for securing me the rights to publish the stories in a book.

Thanks also to Mike Sager, owner, publisher and editor of The Sager Group, for wanting to preserve these stories in a book and make them available to a wider audience. Mike, one of America's most accomplished nonfiction writers working today, launched his young book publishing operation out of a love for fine writing and reporting. I recommend him to everybody writing today. Thanks to University of Illinois journalism graduate student Robert Holly for research. Thanks to Jean McDonald, a journalism faculty colleague at Illinois, for copy editing my Prologue and Epilogue. As ever, thanks to my wife Keran for putting up with me.

Finally, thanks to the people who let me write about them.

ABOUT THE AUTHOR

Walt Harrington was a long-time staff writer for *The Washington Post Magazine,* where he wrote numerous benchmark profiles of notables such as George H. W. Bush, Jesse Jackson, Jerry Falwell and Carl Bernstein, as well as scores of in-depth stories on ordinary people, including a mentally retarded man, a fundamentalist Christian family and a happily married couple. His work has won numerous journalism awards. His book, *The Everlasting Stream: A True Story of Rabbits, Guns, Friendship, and Family,* became an Emmy-winning PBS documentary film. His book, *Crossings: A White Man's Journey into Black America,* won the Gustavus Myers Award for the Study of Human Rights in the U.S. and was declared a vital book on race in America by *The New*

York Times. Mr. Harrington is the author or editor of six other nonfiction books: *American Profiles, At the Heart of It, The Beholder's Eye, Next Wave, Slices of Life,* and *Intimate Journalism*, which has been widely used in journalism classes around the country. He holds master's degrees in sociology and journalism from the University of Missouri and is a journalism professor at the University of Illinois at Urbana-Champaign, where he teaches literary feature writing. His website is WaltHarrington.com.

ABOUT THE PUBLISHER

The Sager Group was founded in 1984. In 2012 it was chartered as a multi-media artists' and writers' consortium, with the intent of empowering those who make art—an umbrella beneath which makers can pursue, and profit from, their craft directly, without gatekeepers. TSG publishes eBooks and paper books; manages musical acts and produces live shows; ministers to artists and provides modest grants; and produces documentary, feature and web-based films. By harnessing the means of production, The Sager Group helps artists help themselves. For more information, please see www.TheSagerGroup.Net.

Made in the USA
Charleston, SC
24 May 2014